Encounter Between Two Worlds

A Journey from Myself to Myself

Louise Illig-Mooncie

BALBOA PRESS
A DIVISION OF HAY HOUSE

Copyright © 2019 Louise Illig-Mooncie.

Interior Graphics/Art Credit: Louise Illig-Mooncie

All rights reserved. No part of this book may be used or reproduced by any means, graphic, electronic, or mechanical, including photocopying, recording, taping or by any information storage retrieval system without the written permission of the author except in the case of brief quotations embodied in critical articles and reviews.

This book is a work of non-fiction. Unless otherwise noted, the author and the publisher make no explicit guarantees as to the accuracy of the information contained in this book and in some cases, names of people and places have been altered to protect their privacy.

Balboa Press books may be ordered through booksellers or by contacting:

Balboa Press
A Division of Hay House
1663 Liberty Drive
Bloomington, IN 47403
www.balboapress.com
1 (877) 407-4847

Because of the dynamic nature of the Internet, any web addresses or links contained in this book may have changed since publication and may no longer be valid. The views expressed in this work are solely those of the author and do not necessarily reflect the views of the publisher, and the publisher hereby disclaims any responsibility for them.

The author of this book does not dispense medical advice or prescribe the use of any technique as a form of treatment for physical, emotional, or medical problems without the advice of a physician, either directly or indirectly. The intent of the author is only to offer information of a general nature to help you in your quest for emotional and spiritual well-being. In the event you use any of the information in this book for yourself, which is your constitutional right, the author and the publisher assume no responsibility for your actions.

Any people depicted in stock imagery provided by Getty Images are models, and such images are being used for illustrative purposes only. Certain stock imagery © Getty Images.

Print information available on the last page.

ISBN: 978-1-9822-2117-1 (sc)
ISBN: 978-1-9822-2119-5 (hc)
ISBN: 978-1-9822-2118-8 (e)

Library of Congress Control Number: 2019901146

Balboa Press rev. date: 02/18/2019

If I were you,
who would I be?
If I were you,
would I still be me?
Whose are those eyes
through which I see?
Looking,
looking back at me?

B. S. J.

A token of Love
dedicated to all those who are
searching for answers and who are
determined to find peaceful solutions.
With deep gratitude to my wonderful family,
my husband Alan and my son Boris for their support
and encouragement to write this book, and to the
next generation, especially my granddaughters
Matilda and Florence.
Wishing you all a light, bright and
peaceful life in a peaceful world!

Contents

1	Start the Day with Peace	1
2	Author's Wish	2
3	The Enemy Within and Reincarnation	8
4	Growing up in Germany	21
5	Working Life and Marriage	30
6	London	38
7	Beginning the Journey	41
8	Meeting M	53
9	Another Emotional Dilemma	61
10	Hardworking Woman	64
11	Healing Journey	70
12	The Story of Al Drucker	76
13	Two More Obstacles and Preparations for India	83
14	Stepping into the Unknown – Indian Diary	90
15	Peace-Story-108	142
16	Epiphany	145
17	Encounter between Two Worlds – From Myself to Myself	149
18	Another Moment Outside Time and Conclusion	158
19	On My Way To The Stars	170
20	Acknowledgments	172

Start the Day with Peace

Sow the Seed of Peace Meditation

Take just a few minutes, every morning, before starting
the journey of your day.
Let your first thought be dedicated to Peace.
Sit in stillness and silence for just a few minutes,
eyes closed, listening and looking within,
breathing gently and evenly.
Then, imagine sowing the Seed of Peace
into a fertile and safe place inside your mind.
Watch it grow.
Watch it spread inside your body,
filling every atom of your being from top to toe.
When you are filled with a sense of Peace, imagine those
peaceful vibrations spreading out into your world.
Say to yourself:
Peace is harmony and balance.
Peace is freedom.
Let peace find a home within me.
Peace is who I am!

Author's Wish

This is my Story – but I am not the Story

I want World Peace! These four words were, for many years, the concluding and possibly winning words at Miss World pageants. Like the sweet song of a blackbird, or a mantra for success, many Miss World contestants have tweeted those magic words out into the TV ether and into living rooms all over the world. As a girl and young woman, I carefully listened to those words with sharpened senses. What will the winner do to achieve this goal? Did anybody ever mention how she would go about it? Nevertheless, I also want world peace, regardless of whether it has been said before or not, regardless of merely repeating an old, worn-out phrase that doesn't seem to be of any consequence to anyone. The fact is, or putting it more softly, *my observation is* that we seem at this moment in time farther away than ever from achieving worldwide peace. Perhaps there will always be warmongers, and there will always be peacemakers. Just now, I guess the balance has tipped towards the warmongers. Therefore, my wish and intention are to make a contribution to peace, the inner and the outer!

What can I do? How can I contribute to a positive outcome? Well, I feel a little bit like an ant trying to climb the highest mountain, but every action starts with the first step. Peace starts with myself! This is my very first step to get my peace mission on the way: I will tell you my story and hope that a spark of inspiration and healing will fly out into the world and make a difference.

Is my story true? Not true? Pure imagination? Wishful thinking? Does it really matter if the story inspires you and the message is intended to be one of love, peace and harmony for this world? Luckily, every word is true! Whatever the contents of this book, this is a genuine account of my experience as someone in a personal and spiritual crisis, and particularly, as a young German who was struggling to come to terms with her country's troubled past. It is about my healing journey, or journey to wholeness, my encounter with an Indian Holy Man, and about another most unusual and unexpected encounter that dramatically changed my life.

It is not always easy to put the most important and influential moments in life into words, especially when those moments are outside the boundaries of what we call *normal*. How can I successfully communicate a message when many of those people who see and hear things that others cannot see and hear are often put away behind secure walls? This is a scary thought, but I have decided to live my life fearlessly, simply because I know that what I've experienced is true for me, and could possibly hold a sense of truth for many others.

After I spoke at a spiritual conference in Dublin some years ago, a well-known doctor of psychiatry approached me. Having heard my talk about my out-of-the-ordinary experience, he broke down in tears in front of a great number of people and asked the heavens for forgiveness. The responsibility for placing many patients who heard voices or saw *departed souls* into psychiatric care, weighed heavily on his conscience. He had dutifully carried out this work until the day he himself had an *out-of-the-ordinary* experience. This challenged everything he'd ever learned and was taught to find a medical or a scientific explanation for. He told me that he would have to resign from his job, as he could no longer believe in his judgment and the rightfulness of his actions.

The pain and guilt he carried were evident. I felt deeply touched by his admission and told him that I hoped he could now find the strength and support to find a new direction in life.

But how justified my initial concerns were, was also perfectly demonstrated by the reaction of an old friend of mine in Germany. I wanted to make the first version of my book (which was entitled *The Jewish Ghost – Being German, A Search for Meaning*) available in Germany, but as my German was undeniably a bit old-fashioned, having lived in the UK for decades, I thought that she would be an excellent candidate to help me with the translation. The first version of my book started with the climax, the reason for writing the book in the first place, which I have now decided to leave for the reader to discover at a much later stage. But my friend fell at the first hurdle. After reading a few pages, she phoned me and asked with annoyance, "Did you take any drugs? Who do you think will believe your story?"

This reaction took me by surprise, as up to this point I had thought that we were on a similar wavelength (for instance, my friend believes in angels, but what I had experienced was obviously a step too far). I felt defensive and hurried to say, "Everything I write about in my book is the result of a genuine and real experience and not the result of having taken some magic pills. I do not have an explanation. Whatever happened to me came out of the blue, without invitation, without being asked for or even longed for. There are things between heaven and earth for which we cannot find an explanation, no matter how hard we try."

A mere "mmm" was her reply, and I felt a huge disappointment about her doubts. I could not imagine working with someone who had no confidence in the subject matter and our attempt to work together on the translation came to an abrupt end. I then wondered: *How would other people react to my book, my very personal experiences, if my own friend is not able to read through the first chapter without thinking that I must have been taking drugs? Surely, there must be hundreds, thousands, or even tens of thousands of people who have had encounters with the spirit world for which they have no explanation?*

After the book had been published, my husband and I went on a brief spa holiday in Germany. This was also a good opportunity for me to present my book to my relatives who lived close to where we stayed. They shocked me with their response. Feeling proud and obviously waiting for positive feedback from those people closest to me, I placed my book in the middle of the coffee table during a visit to my cousin's, hoping that everyone present would jump at the opportunity to open it, read a few lines and say something like, "Well done; looks interesting", followed by a few compliments for having written a book about an extremely sensitive subject in the first place. To my utter amazement, just reading the title must have been enough for my relatives to *scare* them into embarrassed silence. Nobody dared to open my book and flip through the pages. Instead, it was pushed around the table, unopened, like a piece of red-hot coal. I could possibly have come to terms with the situation more easily if this had just happened once, but no, the same behavior was repeated at another cousin's home the next day. Was the subject of the book still too uncomfortable to be discussed? Plenty of food for thought for me and for my husband, who was also a witness to the puzzling conduct of my relatives.

Hours of discussion were to follow between us, trying to make sense and give these otherwise lovely, kind and caring people a good excuse for their strangeness. This was a new experience and utterly alien to me. Aside from not getting a response I could relate to, I felt hurt. I came to the conclusion that perhaps the reaction of my relatives was like a manifestation of all the fears I carried deep inside myself.

Was I looking for a validation for my own story? Was I fearful about sharing what happened to me with others, just in case someone might think that I've been imagining things? Was I worried that I might attract someone's anger by making claims I cannot prove? The answer is *yes*! Even my own upbringing did not allow me to entertain the thought of an experience that cannot be explained.

As chance - or as I would call it, *divine interference* - would have it, a friend of mine pushed the book *The Conversations – 66 Reasons to Start Talking* into my hands, saying, "You may find this interesting". The British author, Olivia Fane, describes in one chapter that her entire family grew up with a completely *natural relationship* to ghosts and a concept of the *other world*. Even Olivia's husband, whom she portrays in her book as a skeptic and nonbeliever with regard to anything supernatural, once had a striking experience on a beach in Norfolk. The encounter happened in broad daylight. This is the story: he was walking along a beach when he saw a fisherman and his boat close by. To his bewilderment, the scenario looked out of time, the boat outdated, and the fisherman's clothes old-fashioned. The image seemed strange. As he stood there, wondering about what he saw, the scene disappeared right in front of his eyes. This left him in a state of shock, but very much intrigued and curious. It did not take long for him to find out that what he had seen was the image of a local fisherman who had gone down with his ship and died in a stormy sea many years earlier.

My heart jumped with joy after reading this story. It catapulted me out of my perceived isolation, and suddenly I had interesting company. I contacted Olivia and thanked her for her book and told her how reading it had given me the confidence to carry on with my book. We arranged a meeting and enjoyed a most interesting afternoon together, talking about life's mysteries, ghosts, and other *close encounters,* naturally.

I came to the conclusion that the British, as a people, have perhaps a much more relaxed relationship with things unexplained and supernatural. After all, the country is famous for its haunted houses, sites, and castles.

For quite some time it has felt as if this book has been asking me to be written. This is a major undertaking for me, as I am not a writer by any means, I am a filmmaker by profession. I am also writing in my second language, English, as all of my important life experiences related to this book, happened while living in England and visiting Ireland. And there is one other, rather strange reason, because somehow I find it easier to voice my feelings in the English language.

However, I can no longer ignore my inner voice, asking to be heard and expressed. I am finally ready and brave enough to claim this space and to take the reader and myself on an intimate and personal journey of self-discovery. My one intention is to promote compassion and understanding and to find answers. I believe that we, the human race, have not found it easy to come any closer to living in peace with each other. It seems to me that whilst there has been progress in many areas of life, such as technology, we have not learned enough from all the suffering that has occurred as a consequence of past conflict. Racial and cultural tensions continue to be experienced almost everywhere and, in my view, they should never become an acceptable part of our daily life.

Marcus Aurelius wrote in his *Meditations* almost 2000 years ago that *...everything is connected with one another, in a Holy bond.*

I also believe in the oneness and connectedness of all things and all beings and in the idea that ultimately, we are one World-family, one breath, one heartbeat.

The Enemy Within and Reincarnation

Sometimes we receive emails that stick out of the crowd and can change our world. Well, a few months ago, a good friend sent such an email to me. This is all it said:

Today I encountered my first enemy, and it was me!

Wow, I thought, why is this touching me so much? I read and re-read this short sentence. What does it mean to me, personally? I started repeating it out loud and then found myself in total agreement with it. For the first time I understood these words on a different level and it felt like a revelation. These are my questions for the reader and my newfound hypothesis *are we, on a sub-conscious level, hooked on the idea of forever having to fight some kind of enemy at our doorstep? And, rather than looking within ourselves, are we tirelessly searching elsewhere for the causes of our troubles? Does an inability to identify ourselves as troublemakers hold us in a state of defense and aggression towards others?*

The Swiss psychoanalyst, C.G. Jung, has an interesting perspective on this human problem.

Everything that irritates us about others can lead us to an understanding of ourselves.

Amazing! So, if you are irritating and annoying me in some way, I am most likely to be irritated and annoyed about those exact characteristics within myself? Food for thought, or not? Why are we not made aware from early childhood of this very important lesson? Why do we instead learn to point our finger and live in disagreement with others?

All this rings a bell for me about my own life and behavior in the past, remembering very well that when facing the breakup of my marriage and then finally the divorce, I disliked and mistrusted the world around me. Most people I came into contact with were scanned with suspicious eyes and from the perspective of a wounded heart. My state of being, my inner pain, was reflecting back at me through the daily experience of life. I met with more quarrels and irritations, less compassion and patience, being over critical of others, etc. I had a bad time with the outside world and with myself. The anger and frustration I felt about my life was crying out to be expressed and released, but my ignorance did not allow me to recognize that I only got back what I gave out to others. I had become my own worst enemy, feeling very sorry for myself indeed.

I can remember some work-related experiences dealing with the same dilemma. I worked for many years, twenty-six to be precise, as a television editor in London. Quite frequently, I had to produce news items and programs about troublesome groups of people who deliberately spread fear and anguish in their communities. They lived out their prejudices as if they were a pastime, a hobby. But a hobby with dangerous and questionable consequences and, sadly, without any concern for the people who had to suffer as a result. How can we explain this need to burst into uncontrolled anger and why does it arise in so many people? How do we fail them, as parents, teachers, guides, perhaps even as friends?

As so often in life, I found someone else expressing this theory about *the enemy within* only a short while after first writing down my own thoughts. The British author, actor and television presenter, Stephen Fry, had lost a few members of his family in the Holocaust. Despite this personal tragedy, he has had a life-long passion for the music of the German composer Richard Wagner, who not only held anti-Semitic views, but whose music was very much liked by Hitler. To find a plausible explanation for his obsession with Wagner, Stephen Fry began a kind of self-experiment. He travelled to Bayreuth in Germany to present a BBC documentary called *Wagner and Me*, aiming to shine a light on the life and work of this controversial composer.

Having supported a failed revolution in Germany, Wagner fled to Zurich in Switzerland in 1848. However, not only did he write most of his magnificent Ring Cycle in exile, but unfortunately, he also wrote an inflammatory, anti-Semitic article entitled *Jewishness in Music*, published in a Leipzig music magazine in 1850. Wagner strongly expressed his prejudice and anti-Semitic attitude and it may be that to this day, this article blemishes Wagner's name and perhaps throws a shadow over his otherwise ingenious work. Surprisingly, Stephen Fry is able to love Wagner, the composer, for his creation of powerful and outstanding works of music. In the documentary he explored Wagner's anti-Semitic feelings and discovered that jealousy was a possible motive. He says, "His (Wagner's) anti-Semitic outburst also had a personal motive: his jealousy towards his celebrated Jewish colleagues Mendelssohn and Meyerbeer".

In an interview with Professor Chris Walton, Wagner expert, historian and author of the book *Richard Wagner's Zurich*, made the point that "Wagner needed to create some kind of major disturbance in his life. He needed some kind of weird kick to get himself going (to be creative). He needed an enemy, or an enemy within himself. He needed to muddy the waters around him in order to write the music that he did."

"Had he only known that his anti-Semitism would only damage himself", Stephen Fry replied.

When I heard this, my mind went into overdrive: *This is it! Could it be said that all of us have a Wagner within us? Do we need the enemy without, to divert us from the enemy within? Do we practice this diversion technique as individuals, as groups and as national stereotypes?* In Wagner's case, the initial reason for his anti-Semitic outburst might have been his intense jealousy towards two successful, contemporary Jewish composers, Felix Mendelssohn and Giacomo Meyerbeer, while he himself was still a struggling, un-established composer. Can the genius be separated from the man? Wagner himself was at the time of his venomous writing relatively unknown and struggling to make ends meet.

A well-known pre-war German conductor, Fritz Busch, who was opposed to Hitler, and was driven from Dresden by the Nazis in 1933, once said, "Es ist wichtiger sich gut zu benehmen, als gute Musik zu machen", **"It is more important to behave well than to make good music"**.

You may not agree with this statement, as it often appears that out of bad behavior or lifestyle comes some great idea or creation. We even make excuses for bad behavior; find it quirky, amusing and entertaining. What is wrong with that, in my eyes, is the fact that someone may get hurt along the way. Is that OK? Sounds as if I am wagging my finger, sitting on a high, moral hobbyhorse, condemning everyone who is not up to *my standards*. Far from it!

I am merely observing, questioning, and exploring, my own level of tolerance when it comes to being a bystander for acts of cruelty. I am also wondering if Wagner would have written even more powerful music had he addressed the *enemy within* himself instead of projecting his fears onto others? We don't know for sure, but what we can say with certainty is the fact that he could have become a more loved person, and his music would not have been tainted with the bad reputation of his character. Wagner's expressions of anti-Semitism surprise us even more, when we find out that he actually had many Jewish friends. About his friendship with the philologist, Samuel Lehrs, he said, "It was one of the most beautiful friendships of my life."

Here we have it again, the duplicity of the human character.

I would like to stress at this point that the projection of intolerance, prejudice and cruelty on to fellow humans is not just the trademark of Germans, although sometimes the British media would like to have us think so. For good and justified reasons, the German people have to deal with this dilemma and try to gradually heal an uncomfortable image that has been attached to them after the Second World War.

But as we look around us, we find examples of Man's inhumanity to Man in all cultures. In the name of science, for example, an American experiment and test program called *MK-ULTRA* was conducted from the early 1950s to the late 1960s against Canadian and US citizens. More than thirty American research institutions and over one hundred scientists were involved in cruel and extensive testing and experimentation on fellow humans, for highly questionable reasons, and in contravention to their human rights. My reason for including the project *MK-ULTRA* as an example of *man's inhumanity to man* is because it all happened in our lifetime and despite the Universal Declaration of Human Rights on the 10th of December 1948.

I feel the need to put this as a question: *How was it possible and acceptable to those in charge, to conduct such brutal and questionable experiments on humans, so shortly after the Second World War with all its expressions of inhumanity, especially the Holocaust? How many more countries did the same?*

This is one aspect of my *quest*, the need to find an answer as to why we inflict suffering or stand by silently and acceptingly as witnesses of suffering. Are we born with awareness and compassion, or do we acquire it along our human journey? What does it take, to turn a human being into a conscious, conscientious, tolerant, kind and all loving being? Many people I know would say that these benevolent human characteristics come with a kind of spiritual awakening.

The well-known New Age author Neale Donald Walsch, received in his channeled work *Conversations with God* a *heavenly* viewpoint about our need to suffer. According to his writings there is an inherent addiction to drama, pain, chaos and suffering in all of us. We apparently *love it*! Although this is hard to imagine, there is perhaps some truth to be found in this. Why would we still be playing the same mindless games, hurting others and ourselves? Is there a way out from running on this spiked treadmill, a way out of living a chaotic, rather than a cosmic life? Can we find a solution to be sometimes, or even permanently connected with everything that is pure love and wisdom?

Jesus undoubtedly tried to show us a way out of suffering. Did he not say, *"Love thy neighbor as you love yourself?"*

There perhaps lies the problem and the tragedy. How many people love themselves for who and what they are?

Jesus tried to guide us in the right direction and so did many enlightened teachers before and after Him. The Buddha suggests meditation as a solution to many of our problems. Currently, there is a strong revival of the Buddha's method for liberation, by addressing issues surrounding the *enemy within* us. Thousands of lives are being transformed, for example, through the practice of Vipassana, or Silent Sitting. This gentle practice of focusing on the simple act of breathing has a most powerful effect on the way we think and feel about ourselves and how we live our lives.

There are an endless number of religious and spiritual paths to walk in order to find what we have always been looking for, our true Self. Strangely, our true Self is always present, it has never left us; it has not gone on vacation to some remote island or a faraway star in the universe. It has always been and always will be present!

This raises the question: *Why do we have such difficulties in finding it? Is the reason for our predicament and seemingly endless search, because we are trying ever so hard to find ourselves outside ourselves?*

The second aspect of my search is the question: *Is there such a thing as reincarnation?* is naturally more complex and difficult to answer. How can we get a glimpse into reincarnation and how can we explore the possibility of past lives? How can I get an answer to my personal question: *Was I a Jew in my past life?*

This very complex issue has occupied a large chunk of my thinking over the past twenty years and the answer is not easily conveyed. I have no proof, in the scientific sense, none at all.

All I have is my life experience and this very personal story. I have long internalized and accepted the theory of reincarnation. Not, because I was brought up to believe in such a concept, far from it, I was raised as a Catholic, but because of where my own life journey has taken me. The idea of past lives is as natural as speaking about the weather to some, while others may find it alienating, nonsensical or right out crazy. Some people argue that there can be no such thing as reincarnation: *This is it! One life and then…nothing, eternal void.* It's a possibility, of course.

But what happens when we have an incidental encounter with a soul or spirit? What happens when we have a so-called *Parallel Universe* or *Alternative Reality* experience? Could this be a moment of tapping into the oneness of all things? Could such a meeting be like a crossing over the timeline and transcending our normal experience of time and space? Surely, the person experiencing an encounter of this kind must be touched to the core. Their thoughts about life may be changed forever and indeed about death, for that matter.

Wouldn't it be fantastic, if we could easily remember, or, at least tap into the memory bank of past lives and draw conclusions from past experiences, mistakes and successes? We may possibly act and think differently. We may be more compassionate towards others, more tolerant, more forgiving, if we only knew for certain that we have been around time and time again, a soul migrating through many circumstances.

> Forms may vary,
> but the indwelling spirit is
> One and the same in All.
> Hence you should bear no ill will
> towards Anyone.
>
> Sai Baba

But why should understanding our life journey be an easy task? Where would the excitement be, the challenges, joys, pains, the search and longing for a greater purpose?

Of course, I have solid proof that I was born as a German citizen in 1949, my birth certificate, parents, passport and 21 years of my life spent living in Germany. What, however, could confirm that I may have been a Jew, a young man, whose life was obviously cut short at about the age of twenty as a consequence of the Holocaust?

I hope that by making the statement that I, a German, may have been a Jew in a past life will not offend any members of the Jewish community. This is certainly not my intention and I sincerely hope that the content of this book will be understood from the heart. This is not an attempt to ease my conscience, make excuses for myself, or others, for being a German with considerable guilt problems, or to gloss over such a painful recent history and finding an escape route by claiming that *'I was possibly Jewish in a past life'*. None of that applies! In the English Dictionary 'guilt' is defined as *'a feeling of worry or unhappiness that you have because you have done something wrong, such as causing harm to another person'*. For a large part of my life I felt *'guilty'* for no apparent reason, for something I hadn't personally done, but which weighed heavily on my shoulders. This feeling propelled me to inquire and search for answers. Without this *guilt*, I may have lived a life in deep, unconscious slumber, without ever asking questions about the meaning and mysteries of life. I somehow doubt this, but it's a possibility. Stronger than anything I could fear from the outside world is my inner voice, which keeps asking me to be heard, telling me to trust and believe in what I have experienced. To trust that what I have to say may help or inspire someone. I once read that if we help and inspire only one other being to live a better, more peaceful life, our life was worth living.

My personal belief is that we have been born and re-born time and time again into different races, cultures, sometimes as male, other times as female, or, both sexes combined in one. There is plenty of evidence to be found for reincarnation from people who remember one, or even several past lives. Some can recall very specific details, including names and places. The information given under hypnosis or some other past-life recall session can often be checked and verified.

A few years ago, the BBC broadcast a series of documentaries about a number of children and adults who remembered a past life, or lives, in great detail. An American psychologist, who was invited as an independent expert to check the validity of the children's claims, had compiled and recorded over 2500 case studies. Presently, there seems to be an ever-increasing number of children being born, who do remember one or even several lifetimes.

The case of a little boy, who miraculously remembered his name and other details from a past life, had touched me deeply. Already as a toddler, he showed a strong interest in fighter planes and was quite obsessive in his behavior, relishing in playing war games. His father became terribly concerned about the boy's sanity, after he began to speak in no uncertain terms about having been someone else in another life. Various therapies were employed to *cure* the child of his symptoms, but to no avail; nothing would change his story. He kept repeating the same name and some kind of identity number. Finally, and in desperation, the father took his son seriously and began to do some research. He found out that the name and number truly existed, it was an air force identity number. He also found a photograph of a smiling, handsome pilot, whom the child identified as himself; and he learned that this young pilot had been shot down in the last war. The memory of this sudden and tragic death remained as a strong imprint in the boy's mind, but, with the help of his father, he was finally able to lay the experience to rest and be at peace with it.

And then, of course, there is the Tibetan tradition of identifying the next Dalai Lama. These beings seem to come into the world with a clear remembrance of their previous life, for example, what kind of items belonged to them: a rosary, walking stick, a drum, a set of false teeth, spectacles or a begging bowl. It has been the custom in Tibet to send out a search team of monks to locate the next incarnation of the Dalai Lama and, when finally found, the child then has to identify various objects from groups of similar type objects, that may have belonged to him in a past life. The author, Mary Craig, describes in her book *Kundun* one particular incident that surprised even the mother of the current Fourteenth Dalai Lama.

Apparently, after his arrival in Lhasa, Tibet, the four-year-old boy had mysteriously insisted that his teeth were in a certain house within the Norbulingka Park. He was taken inside the house and pointed to a box, claiming that this was where he left his teeth. The box was opened and it was found to contain a set of dentures that used to belong to the Thirteenth Dalai Lama.

How can we make sense of these experiences and why would we have many or, as some believe, even hundreds of lifetimes? Perhaps we are here to sample all of life's rich tapestry. Once we have done this and we have played our parts well, like actors in a play, learning and understanding everything that needs to be learned, as a thief or saint, a prostitute or nun, tyrant or savior, we merge into the great oneness by dropping our ego-riddled self-identification.

The question still remains as to who has invented this *school of life* and all the different roles and games we get to play. Who is the designer of the Divine drama? Or do we get to design our own lesson plan?

It was always relatively easy for me to believe in a grander pattern, whose designer and playwright is the invisible, unfathomable, Divinity, or God, whichever name or form you give Him or Her and of which we all are part. Nurtured by my own experiences, this belief has gained momentum and has strengthened over the years, proving valid and healing to me. It is not my intention to preach a particular doctrine or to promote a certain guru. Far from it! I believe that there is a *tailor-made* path for each one of us, as individual as our DNA, but that we are ultimately all one, all part of the same family. We may therefore be able to break down the boundaries, which hold us in hostile resentment of others and potentially separate us from people of other races, cultures, religions and beliefs.

All over the world there are efforts being made by people to demonstrate that living a life in harmony and peace with one and all is a possibility.

One of my heroes is the Jewish conductor, pianist and peace activist Daniel Barenboim. His *West-Eastern Divan Orchestra* (named after an anthology of poems by the German writer, Goethe) is in my opinion a brilliant example of the expression of tolerance and compassion, as the orchestra consists of Muslims, Christians and Jews. It inspires peaceful solutions to conflict in a lighthearted way, and, with the help of music, Barenboim tried and still tries to reconcile warring factions. He and the late American-Palestinian literary scholar, Edward Said, founded the ensemble in 1999, consisting of around one hundred mainly Arab and Israeli orchestra members. However, in 2011, Barenboim had to find a number of non-Israeli musicians for his Peace Concert on the Gaza Strip. Being Jewish, he himself was at first not given permission to attend, but after a lengthy period of negotiation with the Palestinian authorities, and stubborn insistence on his part, he was finally allowed to conduct his own orchestra on the Gaza Strip. The beautiful sound of music by Mozart was played on Palestine soil, although under heavy security, contributing in a wonderful way to World Peace.

A few months later, Barenboim travelled with his orchestra to South Korea, to improve and promote the inter-Korean dialogue between North and South. Barenboim says that for him music is not an escape from reality. On the contrary, he believes that he can, with the help of music, create a *bigger reality*, as music transcends all man-made boundaries and helps to lift the human spirit. Barenboim continues his *peace mission* with concerts all over the world.

Another contribution to reconciliation and world peace recently caught my eye, as there is a strong connection to my own story. A *Week of Brotherhood* (Woche der Brüderlichkeit) has taken place in Germany every year since 1952. After very small and almost unnoticed beginnings, the event has developed into a nation-wide celebration, promoting dialogue and understanding between the Christian and Jewish communities in Germany. I had never heard of it. By the time I had left Germany to live in the UK, in the mid-1970s, the event was not yet well publicized by the media, not much *noise* was being made about it. And in England, I had never come across an article or a news story about it. *Good news usually doesn't travel as well and fast as bad news,* I concluded.

But this is how I found out: I was sitting at home, in the UK, channel-hopping and literally by chance stumbling over a news item about the *Week of Brotherhood* celebrations in Augsburg, Germany. Internally all stirred up, I sat glued to my TV screen, watching a festive gathering of Jews and Germans, aiming to promote friendship and to continue looking to the future with hope and goodwill on both sides. The genuine and heartwarming generosity of spirit amongst all the people present spilled over into my living room, hundreds of miles away from the actual event, and it filled me with a sense of happiness.

I was deeply moved about the fact that such an amazing platform for reconciliation had been created, and by the unifying words of many high profile Jewish and German speakers. *This is a wonderful opportunity for healing the past,* I thought.

One sentence from Rabbi Henry Brandt's speech at the conference left a deep mark:

"Wir möchten einen breiteren Horizont setzen, über den Tellerrand hinaus blicken."
"We would like to set a wider horizon, looking beyond the edge of our plate."

Yes, that is exactly what I believe, what I hope for, wish for. I hurried to write down this sentence in my diary. We have to start seeing a wider picture for our world, otherwise, what kind of world do we leave to the next generations?

When we forgive,
The past no longer controls us.

(Unknown)

Growing up in Germany

I was born in Germany, this lifetime, in September 1949. Mainz, the town I grew up in, founded by the Romans over 2000 years ago, lay largely in ruins from the consequences of the Second World War. My hometown had been an Allied Forces prime target, as it had two bridges of strategic importance crossing over the River Rhine. It was also a military key point, connecting the counties of Hessen and Rhine Palatinate.

I remember the beautiful baroque church *St. Peter* with a gaping hole in the roof and with its interior treasures exposed to the elements, the grand castle of the Kurfürst (Prince Regent), the museum and the once quaint houses around the market place opposite the cathedral all largely in ruins…those were strong images of my childhood (I am happy to say that over a long period of time many of these great buildings have been beautifully restored). I have very clear memories of holding on to my parents' hands as a little girl, a feeling of fear having a solid grip on me, walking past heaps of rubble and bombed-out buildings in the center of town. There was destruction all around us, even in the mid to late 1950s.

But whatever it was that had happened here, nobody was keen to talk about it or to answer my questions. War was not talked about very often during my childhood and while I was growing up. Not even in my history lessons at school. A *conspiracy of silence* prevailed for years to come. Strangely enough, we seemed to race through the subject of the Second World War with such a speed that only a few key words, names and dates, like 1939 to 1945, remained stuck in my mind. There was always an air of embarrassment around this subject. I learned and knew more about the 18th century French Revolution or any other period in history.

My classmates also confirmed this impression to me during our first school reunion in 2006. I had to find out and I asked everyone present:

"Did I, did we, hear about the Holocaust during our school days?"

The answer was negative. Surely, we would have remembered if we had heard that millions of Jews were killed deliberately, systematically and most cruelly in our country during the Third Reich? I would have been horrified, traumatized and haunted by nightmares. A child would never forget hearing about such an atrocity. However, I have no such recollection and truly believe that this darkest time of German history was deliberately kept a secret from us by our parents, teachers, politicians; in fact, by all adults around us. I conclude that the reason for keeping this part of the past *under wraps* is easy to understand: *not enough time had elapsed since the nightmare had ended. It was all still too raw and uncomfortable for the post-war generation to mention the war, perhaps to even think about its awfulness.*

The conspiracy of silence throughout German society was endorsed by the politician, Konrad Adenauer, the first German chancellor after the war. He wanted Germany to be able to start afresh and leave the memories of the war behind. Therefore, he decided that the Holocaust was not to be part of the school curriculum. *Aha…I thought, no wonder my generation shared the same gap of knowledge with regard to the Second World War.*

My father, born in 1925, was just 18 years old when he was called up in 1943 to join the German Army. Perhaps it was his stroke of luck that the Americans captured him shortly afterwards. He had spent most of the war years as a prisoner of war in the United

States (Mississippi-Missouri), where he contracted malaria. In 1945, after the war had ended, he was transferred to England and given a job on a farm near Reading. He was finally sent home in 1948. I remember him saying that he felt *robbed of his youth* and I believe that this realization made him quite a bitter, unbalanced person; forever chasing the good life after the war was over, to make up for lost years.

I was almost 30 years old when my father volunteered for the first time in my life to speak about his wartime experiences. Perhaps a glass of wine too many loosened his tongue and jogged his memory on one particular evening. I had the impression that these memories were still very painful. He described vividly how he and other prisoners of war were treated in the American prison camp:

"The German captives were given hardly any food to eat over long periods of time. Some of the American soldiers or prison guards would stand behind the fence eating their food, and then just throwing a few leftovers to a great number of hungry men. The inevitable fight between us was then watched gleefully, like a dog fight."

It still saddens my heart to think that my father was almost starving and was treated with such cruelty. What are your thoughts? If you are not German, do you think: *serves them right for starting the war in the first place*, or do you feel compassion for those suffering men, even though they are German? How would you feel if one of your loved ones had to go through such an experience?

My father did not want the war, just like millions of other Germans, young and old, who had no choice in the matter. He wanted to live out his life and his dreams, not the crazy ideas of a madman, Adolf Hitler, and his equally misguided followers.

Louise's parents, Heidi & Josef, 1949

My mother, also born in 1925, grew up in a small village in the Moselle valley, in the southwest of Germany. Her family lived mainly from wine-making farming and keeping a few farm animals. She too was to suffer, as her favorite brother became an early casualty of the war in 1939. He was only 23 years old.

Her father, the grandfather I have never met, was 58 when the war started. Sadly, he died in 1939 from pneumonia, only two weeks after the death of his youngest son. The family doctor lived only a few miles away, but he was unable to reach their village, as the German Army was marching toward France and all the roads were blocked by military traffic.

My grandmother was left with four youngsters, three teenage girls and another son who had also been called up to fight in the war.

What keeps us going in times of tragedy?

I feel the need to give you some of my family background, just in case you may be tempted to think that my relatives were Nazis, and that as a consequence, I had to deal with a guilty conscience on their behalf. This is definitely not the case, although, if it were the case, what difference would it have made? I felt guilty anyway! But luckily for me, there are no wartime skeletons in the family cupboard. In fact, I always wondered if my grandmother on my father's side had a Jewish connection. I know nothing about her, neither does my mother; there is no one I could ask about her, I never met a relative or knew where she came from. She was just there, with her long ebony hair tied in a bun and her dark brown eyes. She will always be a mystery.

Anyway, war seemed like a dirty word and my parents and everyone else in the country had to get on with life. Like a phoenix rising from the rubble of wartime, they worked and worked and worked for a new beginning.

Although I grew up in ignorance of the extent of evils perpetrated by the Third Reich throughout the 1930s and 40s, I sensed a restless unease and franticness around me, compensated by an exaggerated lust for life. Gigantic portions of rich, fatty, buttery, creamy food and an excess of alcohol seemed to be the rule. And if those indulgences weren't enough, a wave of sexual freedom swept over Germany like a tsunami, bringing chaos to the nation's health and family life. I don't wish to be overcritical, knowing very well how traumatizing the experience of war must have been for everyone, but perhaps I, my generation, was also traumatized by post-war goings-on. Only now, decades later, can I see with some clarity and an open, more understanding mind that not all was well with the behavior of the adults around me and the standards with which I was brought up.

As for me, the observer, I developed a passion very early in life for everything to do with India, its culture and traditions, and for justice, politics and for the wellbeing of all people and creatures, and an almost desperate hunger to find answers to the puzzles of life.

My upbringing at home was without prejudice. People around me were only divided into the categories *lovable and keep close,* or *not so lovable and therefore keep your distance.* They were never divided into shades of skin color, religion or cultural backgrounds. For this aspect of my education I am eternally grateful to my family, as it had a very positive influence on how I lived and still live my own life.

In fact, when I was a little girl, in the 1950s, I enjoyed growing up and playing with a boy of my own age, from a nearby Gypsy community. My dear grandfather, who was a baker and cake maker by profession, provided the Gypsies with food from our bakery. I fondly remember their kindness and warmth towards me. Their caravans with hand-painted designs and vivid colors must have left a deep impression on me, as I love everything bright and beautiful. Yes, they positively influenced my childhood and I cherish my memories of this wonderful community.

Sadly, my friend passed away. I never knew what had happened to him. All I remember is that at the age of about four or five, I was walking in a procession behind a small coffin. Grieving people all around me, wailing and sobbing their hearts out. This was quite an unsettling experience for me. Where was my friend? Why did he go away and where did he go? At the time, I did not understand any of the drama. The only thing I knew was that I had lost something precious.

When I was growing up, my biggest personal battle was fought with the Catholic Church and the inner conflicts and confusion arising from my religious education. There was no evidence in my world that the existence of the Ten Commandments turned human beings into better people. The church, at the time, appeared to be advocating a severe, sexually repressive and overly strict doctrine that made people fear, and not love God. As a child, I certainly feared God and His apparent need for punishment, even for the tiniest of sins, like secretly taking a biscuit out of the cookie jar, or doing a detour past the sweet shop after school. Observing adults around me, listening carefully to stories my parents and grandparents gossiped about, I came to the conclusion that many people did not mind lying or betraying this God they did not love.

Not to mention the priest in our local church who was, in

my eyes, only *blessed* with a foul temper, prejudice, a total lack of compassion and high blood pressure. Unfortunately, he was in charge of my religious education. I skipped church frequently to avoid his teachings of fire and brimstone and often, his moralizing comments against our family business, preached from the pulpit and sometimes in the presence of my parents, grandparents and myself. That's why I skipped Mass on Sundays; I could bear it no longer. But our priest, who was also my religious teacher in school, punished me for my behavior on the following Monday mornings. After reducing me to tears in front of the class, he made me stand, facing the wall, for the entire duration of our religious studies lesson. This went on for years, until I changed to another school. I can now confidently say that this was counterproductive on his part, as it turned me into a rebel and a critic of the Catholic Church. However, and I need to write this to *balance the books*, I have great admiration and respect for the current head of the Catholic Church, Pope Francis. He is, in my eyes, a perfect example of a true Christian as he lives what he preaches; he is *walking his talk*. I wish I had met people like him when I grew up!

Louise, aged 9, at school

This was my problem: My parents and grandparents were proprietors of two local cinemas in Mainz. Strangely enough, my grandparents' cinema was in an old, converted Protestant church. Movies like *Cat on a Hot Tin Roof* with Elizabeth Taylor or *La Dolce Vita* with Anita Ekberg or just about any film with Marilyn Monroe were a thorn in our priest's side. Although I was only a child, I knew the implications of his sermons. Nobody in the congregation would dare to be seen going to either of our cinemas and my family suffered financial loss as a consequence. Like all Catholic girls aged 10 or 11, I had to go to my first confession before attending Holy Communion. I remember strong feelings of fear arising in me, especially because I felt extremely uncomfortable with our priest. What if the ground opens up beneath my feet and I go straight to hell, there and then, without ever seeing my family and friends again? While waiting for my turn to absolve myself of this vast array of sins which I had supposedly committed, and which I had scribbled in shaky handwriting on a small piece of paper, my body trembled and my bladder emptied into my pants. I had reached crisis point!

I ask you, the reader: *What sin could a child of 10 possibly commit to end up in such a crisis?* Well, perhaps I shouldn't have been hiding my best friend's favorite doll under my bed? I had skipped church the previous Sunday and gone for a walk instead? Was going to the movies really a sin? Whatever my *crimes*, I do not think anyone should feel so intimidated and live with the burden of fear and guilt for what are mere trivialities. Perhaps my recurring nightmare about turning up in church inappropriately dressed and being punished for it deeply reflected the extent of my insecurities.

I am still trying to make sense of some of my experiences as a Catholic. For example, I remember a huge 8ft fence being erected around our schoolyard, just to stop us from meeting our Protestant friends from a nearby school at break-time. Why stop Catholic youngsters from making friends with Protestants? What did our teachers fear? Were they concerned that we might be contaminated, polluted for life, just like the fallout after a nuclear explosion? As no explanation was ever given to us, we continued to disobey orders, when we could.

The biggest sin at the time was to go out with or worse, to fall in love with a Protestant boy, but of course, many of us did. The excitement of having a *sinful kiss* with a Protestant boy was immense and certainly worthwhile going to confession for! I had learned, without great difficulty, the art of sinning and confessing about the small things in life.

Nothing made sense to me in those days. Children and especially teenagers want to understand the actions of adults. Why build a fence, if it has the opposite effect? Why stop Catholic youngsters from making friends with Protestants? Did the so-called *Peace Wall*, a massive dividing line through the heart of Belfast accelerate peace between Protestants and Catholics or has it had the opposite effect?

Unbeknown to me, while I was fighting the demons of my childhood, my family was fighting for financial survival. Television had arrived in many households and it was no longer necessary to move out of your living room armchair into a less comfortable cinema seat to watch movies. We suffered financial losses, resulting in the closure of my parents' and my grandparents' cinema, which was once upon a time a Protestant Church, and was rented out and turned into a graphic design studio. Times of hardship were to follow for my stressed-out parents and grandparents. My lovely grandfather died unexpectedly of a heart attack, caused by high levels of stress and severe economic problems. I was devastated by the loss, as I loved him very much and had always felt closer to him than to my own father. The world had suddenly become a lonelier place. For many years to come I hoped that his death was just a mistake that could be remedied, and that…one day, I would see his face again in the crowd, or on a bus…

We moved to another town and both of my parents found, in time, a new life, a new job…in television. What irony!

Although my personal dream was to become an interior designer, my father had other plans for me. He wanted me to have a financially secure future and not, as he called it, *a penniless life as an artist*. It came as no surprise, that I was to start my professional career in the media too.

Working Life and Marriage

After finishing my education, I trained to become a film editor for a major German broadcaster. My first impressions of the media world left me reeling in a good way. This new world was simply fascinating. Remember that in the late 1960s television was a relatively new employer and anyone who was lucky enough to work for such a glamorous institution (that's how I perceived it) felt a bit like a new member of a Royal Household, proud to be part of it.

The frantic pace of work, competitiveness, the pushiness and use of connections within the company, the fashionable display of sarcasm, sexual antics of colleagues, gossip, general stress of deadlines and overindulgence in alcohol, coffee and cigarettes, were perhaps off-putting but generally accepted features about my new working environment. Life seemed to be lived in the fast lane, at least so it appeared to me.

I believe that there are no coincidences and that everything in life turns out as it should. I was obviously in the right job at the right time. After all, interesting and inspiring people, who others only saw on their TV screens at home, happened to be my work colleagues. This aspect was an attractive compensation, especially for the long and irregular working hours.

The fact that television was responsible for my parents' financial difficulties was no longer an issue. *All's well that ends well*, as Shakespeare has it. I love that phrase. My entire family, as well as me, had found employment and financial security after a long spell of hardship, by actually working for the media.

I was still a newcomer, aged 19, and only a few months into my newfound employment, when a well-known TV film director and author (I will abbreviate his name and call him H.D.) approached me while I was queuing for a sandwich in our canteen. He was a much admired, gossiped about, larger than life, mysterious and interesting figure of small stature. A very groomed, often stroked Karl Marx-type beard made him look sophisticated and handsome in an odd sort of way. Women chased him in droves. In fact, I had hardly ever seen him without a female entourage. When he approached me, he was miraculously on his own.

"You look to me like Heinrich Heine's muse", he said, not wasting any time on niceties or introducing himself to me. He presumed that I knew him.

"I am going to produce a TV documentary about Heinrich Heine and I would like you to play the part of his muse. I've been watching you for some time and I believe that you are the right person in looks and character to portray her".

I stood as if lightning had struck me. *Things like this only happen to others, I* thought. My mind quickly scanned its grey cells in search of Heinrich Heine: German Jew by birth, 179? - 185? (don't remember the exact dates) - inspired Karl Marx and Nietzsche with his political writings - wrote very beautiful romantic prose - is one of my favorite poets - exiled himself to Paris because he disagreed with German politics - died of syphilis which he caught from the washerwomen in Paris - his body fell apart while his mind stayed sharp and acute to his last breath - was one of the many proscribed authors during the Third Reich as his critical views about Germany still rang the uncomfortable bells of truth almost one hundred years later.

What do I say to H.D.? Should I tell him that I do not have the self-confidence to play such a part, that he must have made a mistake, that perhaps I am not pretty enough to be anyone's muse? An opportunity like this may never come again. Heart pounding and short of a spectacular response, I timidly agreed to his proposal. He informed me that he would contact my superiors to ask for me to have some time off work for filming the two-part documentary series and that we should meet up soon to discuss everything in detail. Lastly he said:

"And by the way, make sure you have a valid passport. We are going to Paris."

It was almost impossible to contain my excitement. I wanted to explode, tell the world what had happened to me just then, and call my friends, parents and everyone in my phonebook. I believe that all eyes were on us during our short encounter in the canteen, as he always took center stage when he walked into a room. I collected myself together, which was not an easy task, and finally queued up to buy my sandwich, fully aware that the heat in my cheeks must have reached boiling point and that the red-hot color in my face was there for everyone to see. Never mind, this was my moment and I cherished every second of it.

My adventure started several weeks later, travelling to Paris and other places of significance for the film project. A fantastic period of learning, observing, challenging myself, of expanding mentally, emotionally and being exposed to ideas previously alien to me about art, culture and politics had started a new chapter of my life. H.D. played the role of a mentor and I learned to understand why so many people, male and female, were seeking and loving his company. He was a genius storyteller, full of charm and with a very sharp mind. It is possibly easy to read between the lines that he fascinated and impressed me profoundly.

One evening in Paris, the entire team was invited to a splendid meal in one of the many pretty Montmartre restaurants. H.D. felt compelled to tell us the intriguing story of his life:

His mother fell in love with a German Jew and became pregnant whilst unmarried. The real father sadly abandoned the pregnant woman and moved away. Luckily for her, a high-ranking German officer felt sorry her and the unborn child and proposed marriage. This ultimately must have saved H.D's life, as nobody questioned his Aryan status when he was called up to join the army in 1939, as a young man. A few years into his military service, he realized the evils being committed by the Third Reich. He joined a resistance group and helped to plot a coup against Hitler. The coup was foiled. He was caught, ended up in prison and was to be executed by a firing squad. Somehow it came to light that he was actually Jewish. He was transferred from a prison to a concentration camp and locked up in a cage, not able to stretch his legs for about four weeks.

What stopped him from going insane, from giving up and losing his will to live was the extraordinary fact that he started seeing beautiful visions of Christ.

"These visions of Christ sustained me", H.D. said, "They made me forget my pain and discomfort for a while."

He said he would spare us the finer details of what he witnessed in the concentration camp and of his own physical and mental condition. H.D. came close to death's door. The horror of that time still tormented him, especially at night. He was rescued by Allied Forces pushing into Germany and lived to tell the story.

"I am still haunted by nightmares', he said with a solemn voice, '…and they are getting more horrific all the time. I hardly ever sleep".

Silence. I did not know what to say, what to think. It was obvious, neither did the others. Everyone sipped nervously on a glass of wine, eyes down. In shame?

This was the first time I had heard of such a personal tragedy, heard about the horror of concentration camps. My heart was aching. What kind of national legacy was I born into? What did it mean to be a German? Do others hate us for committing such a crime? How can I now hold my head up high and be proud of who I am and where I come from? No conclusion could be arrived at that evening. H.D. managed to turn the subject for discussion totally on its head, steered us cleverly from tragedy to light entertainment and the dual role of washerwomen during Heinrich Heine's stay in Paris. For the rest of the evening, he kept us amused with his endless stream of interesting stories. Truth or fiction? I never found out.

Louise with film crew at Montmartre Cemetery, Paris

Naturally, being a young woman, Montmartre Cemetery, where Heine was buried, was not my favorite place of work, especially on a grey, overcast and gloomy day. The flower decorations on the graves were mostly made of plastic, but all glory and color, if there ever was any, had faded away. In my eyes, at the time, it all looked quite spooky, like the set of a Bollywood horror movie (although, years later I visited the cemetery again and had no such impressions; on the contrary, I found it in parts peaceful, poetic and beautiful). My face must have reflected the gloomy mood of the sky and our surroundings, as I managed the perfect look required for the film. The film crew showered me with praise after finishing the shoot at Montmartre Cemetery, and H.D. thought that I did really well, considering that this was my first time in front of a film camera. It appeared that only I knew how much the environment helped me with my limited acting talents.

Looking back at this time of my life, I can see the slow unraveling of my German/Jewish life story, the piecing together of a mighty puzzle. Was it mere coincidence that I was part of a film about Heinrich Heine, a Jew, and that my mentor and friend H.D. was also a German Jew and that he had told us his incredible life story?

I can sum up this section of the book with the words of the German poet and philosopher Friedrich Schiller:

There is no such thing as chance; and what seems to us merest accident, springs from the deepest source of destiny.

Returning to my *normal work* at German TV only happened with great reluctance. My brief *outing* as an actress, as a muse, was most enjoyable and will always have a special place in my memories.

Only two years into my career I fell head over heels in love with a colleague. It was love at first sight when we met at our company's annual outing. We married within one year and seemed a perfect match for each other for a great number of reasons. Our interests in Buddhism, meditation, poetry, spirituality, music and our work in the media created a strong bond between us at first. I imagined that this bond would be like a protective shield against life's challenges.

Unfortunately, my husband's job demanded a fair amount of travelling around Europe and we spent most of the first year of our young married life apart. This was a difficult situation for us, as film crews in general had a bad reputation. They were not renowned for being faithful to their partners. Lurid stories about affairs circulated in our office like wildfire. I disliked the phone calls I received from my husband late in the evening from some restaurant or bar far away. I wanted a *normal* marriage, where husband and wife would have cozy evening meals together, by candlelight. But then, I was only twenty-two years old.

Along came a job offer my husband could not refuse. This new turn of events looked like the answer to all of my prayers. He was offered a position in the London-based office of German Television. We were hoping that moving to England would be like a new beginning for our young marriage, that we could spend lots of time together and not be separated by frequent faraway trips.

Unfortunately for me, I had to resign from my own job, as there was no vacancy for an editor in London. I would only be able to work on a temporary freelance basis. This was the plight of professional women at the time. Many of us had to give up our careers as we followed our husbands into another country and an uncertain future.

With growing awareness
our vision will become clearer.
Those who only search outside themselves
may get lost in the search.
Those who look inside for the truth,
Awaken!

L. I-M

6

London

Kings Road, Chelsea, Carnaby Street, Portobello Road, Knightsbridge and Mayfair, here I come. The office of German Television was in the heart of Mayfair, just off the famous Berkeley Square (in between Hyde Park and Piccadilly Circus) where, according to an old British song, the nightingales sing. It was hugely exciting for me to explore London and to recognize places I had only seen in magazines or on television. I shall never forget my first purchase: a pair of multi-colored, dangerously high platform shoes, bought in Carnaby Street. English fashion was so much more vibrant and outrageous than anything I had seen in Germany. None of my German friends would be seen dead in a clothes combination of pink and purple or red and green, but here in London, everything was possible. The streets were paraded by birds of paradise and I would happily sit in a cafe for a good while, just staring at all the colorful passers-by.

I loved the freedom of expression, the madness, individualism, eccentricity and non-conformism. People appeared to have a greater personal freedom, seemed less judgmental about the appearance of others. Perhaps I saw life in the UK with rose-tinted glasses, because of a much more austere upbringing in Germany in the 1950s and 1960s? Whatever the reason for my enthusiasm, the *British way of life* just bowled me over. Everything I saw made a great impression.

At least once a week we would get dressed up to go to the theater or a concert in the Royal Albert Hall or some other great venue. I would wear a long evening dress and my husband a dark suit, white shirt and bow tie. How times have changed, now you can go anywhere in jeans and jumper. I make no judgment on what is better, but I do recall having fun dressing up for the evening.

Moving to London also meant lots of partying. Quite contrary to other major cities around the world, London appeared to go to sleep after 11pm (in the early 1970s at least). However, behind closed doors, people defeated this sleepy city and made up for its lack of nightlife by throwing lots and lots of parties.

To my surprise, fancy dress was a highly popular activity. In Germany, dressing up in such a way is done only in the Carnival season, starting eleven minutes after the 11th hour, in the 11th month every year and ending on Ash Wednesday. But in London, it was fancy dress time all year round. The theme of *Vicars and Tarts* seemed to be one of the most popular ways of dressing up at the time. I often wondered what this said about the nation's sexual habits, fancies and fantasies.

Another eccentric habit was the brewing of everything I knew in Germany as fruit salad, and turning it into a lethal concoction called fruit wine, certain to give you a massive headache and hangover. Good wine was hard to come by for those with a small budget and almost everyone I met had turned into an amateur wine-maker, with equipment stacked in bedrooms, larders and even living rooms. For my professional winemaking relatives on the River Moselle, this was shocking and amusing news.

Admittedly, I found London quite overwhelming. The sheer size of the city, the rush hour, masses of people to-ing and fro-ing, the time one would spend in traffic jams, trying not to be late for work, theatres, doctor's appointments and so on, all contributed to a hectic and crazy lifestyle.

I never forget being stuck in a traffic jam with an urgent news item intended for the early evening news (German TV had no broadcasting facilities of their own in those days). To the astonishment and horror of my taxi driver I got out of the car in the middle of a traffic jam in Oxford Street, hailed down a passing motorbike, asked the driver to take me to ITV in Great Portland Street for the transmission of the news item to Germany. He grinned and took on the challenge. I held on tight to a total stranger while praying furiously for our safety. Miraculously, we made it on time, but what a stressful nightmare it had been.

Little did I know that by choosing to be in England, I was to embark on an amazing journey of self-discovery, and little did I know that I would only reach my destination about twenty years later.

England was to become my spiritual home.

Beginning the Journey

One of my husband's colleagues was a wild, wonderful and very funny Jewish man in his late twenties, married to a stunning, long-haired, Kate Bush-type looking woman, also Jewish. They invited us to a birthday party in their home in North London.

During the evening I started chatting to one of the guests and found out that he was also Jewish, in fact, so were most of the guests.

I suppose the question "… and where do you come from?" had to arise during some point of any conversation. My ability to express myself in the English language was still a bit clumsy and awkward. It was easy to detect that I was a foreigner.

When I answered, "I'm German", the young man's face turned into an angry grimace and he unloaded the full blast of his anger against the Germans there and then. He told me about the dreadful atrocities committed by my fellow countrymen and all the suffering they had inflicted on the Jewish community. His family had also suffered. My heart started pounding and I burst into tears. Nothing like this had ever happened to me. I felt so incompetent, so lost, at that moment. How to respond to this situation? My mind was desperately searching for the right words, the right response.

"Yes, I know, the Holocaust was horrific. I'm sorry, so sorry. But my father didn't kill or discriminate against Jews, nor did my grandfather. On the contrary, my grandfather helped to protect vulnerable people. He gave food and support to local Gypsy families during and after the war. He himself suffered from severe asthma and was not called up to fight for Germany. My father was only fourteen years old in 1939, when the war started. He was not a Nazi either...".

Nothing I said appeased the young man. I was fast running out of words and excuses. My head was racing. I understood that he had reasons to be angry, but why was he angry with me? What had I done and how could I be forgiven?

Whatever I said fell on deaf ears. I retreated into the toilet and cried my eyes out. My husband was totally unaware of my crisis and obviously not sharing the same experience at all. He was enjoying himself. It was my problem alone, but why? This was only the beginning of a painful and soul-searching journey, forcing me to question my whole existence in relation to the fact that I was born a German (in this life-time).

Why did I never question what had happened during the last war? Did I subsequently and subconsciously feel guilty? Did I carry some of the burden of the German collective unconscious, as C. G. Jung might have put it? Was I scared to find out the truth? That night changed the rest of my life.

Suddenly, I noticed that British television was full of anti-German programs. Almost every night one could see *ze Germans* goose-stepping over the country's television screens. The nation was bombarded, and still is, with documentaries, films and comedies about the Second World War.

My observations started to possess me and I took everything I heard, read and saw very personally. I now know that this was all part of my journey. People say that the last thing you learn about a language is its sense of humor. I can only confirm this, as I totally failed to see the funny side of well-loved English comedy programs like *Dad's Army* and *Fawlty Towers*. This of course changed over the years. I can now laugh whole-heartedly about the classic *Don't mention ze War* TV sketch, in which the outrageously rude, funny and eccentric hotelier Basil Fawlty was getting away with very insulting behavior towards his German guests, including *Heil Hitler* salutes.

And I can laugh about the Germans too. For example the odd fact that my countrymen have a very bad reputation amongst British holiday makers. They are known to race to the hotel swimming pool at 5 am in countless holiday resorts all over the world, just to put down a towel in order to secure their place in the sun, next to the pool for the rest of the day. I always thought that this was just vicious gossip, until I had first hand experience on a holiday with my son in Lanzarote, one of the Canary Islands. When we arrived at the pool after breakfast, all the deckchairs and spaces had been taken, quietly occupied by an array of colorful towels, put down at dawn by German holidaymakers. The mere sight of it made me laugh out loud to the bewilderment of my son, who had not heard of this phenomenon up until that moment. But then, I met British holidaymakers who took baked beans, bacon, pork pies, tea bags and other British foodstuff to France, Spain, Italy…the lands of the most delicious and tasty gourmet cooking. How comprehensible is that?

I guess every nation has strange and amusing little stereotypical habits, but it was my *German-ness*, which embarrassed me more than anything. It is very hard not to take things personally when certain emotions hit you like an avalanche, just because your mind has decided that it is under attack. I remember feelings of insecurity and discomfort creeping in when people asked me where I came from. As my English improved rapidly and my effort not to sound so Germanic seemed to *pay off,* people often thought that I was French or Italian. Never did I contradict them, just in case they didn't like Germans, and to avoid any kind of challenging encounters.

Thank God, I thought, *that I had brown eyes and hair, and was not a blonde and blue-eyed Aryan*. Would it have made matters worse if I had been blonde and blue-eyed? I really don't know, and I doubt it, but ultimately, it made no difference to how I felt about myself. I was in a crisis about my identity and totally embarrassed about my nationality. How could I be proud of my *Fatherland,* proud to say, *I am German*, when asked where I come from? Yet, there is so much to be proud of, starting with great composers, artists, philosophers, and inventors, not to mention beautiful towns, villages, landscapes, and on a smaller scale, my lovely family. Why couldn't and shouldn't I be proud? No answer came from within myself. All I felt was a numb embarrassment and pain.

This was not a topic I would discuss with anyone else, not even with my husband or friends. Whatever it was, it was stirring inside my heart and soul and I did not know at first how to tackle the problem. I am of course emphasizing those aspects of my life, which highlighted my inner and outer difficulties, rather than elaborating on the many wonderful events in between my personal challenges.

But wonderful things did happen too, like the gift of a baby boy. In 1973 our lovely son was born. We named him Boris Siddhartha. Like most young people in those days, we had read Hermann Hesse's book *Siddhartha,* and naming our son after an enlightened being seemed a good idea at the time. The name Boris was inspired by an aristocratic friend of ours who lived in Berlin.

Our happy time together as a family was sadly short-lived. The situation we tried to walk away from in Germany, being separated too often due to my husband's work commitments, followed us to England. The *Troubles* in Northern Ireland flared up in around 1974 and his job demanded that he should go wherever news stories had to be filmed, for example:

> May 1974, three no-warning car bombs exploded in Dublin, killing 26 and injuring almost 300 people;
>
> December 1974 Birmingham Pub bombings, killing 21 people and injuring 182;
>
> 1975 turned into *one of the bloodiest years of the conflict.*

As a wife and mother, I was scared. Being a cameraman was becoming a very dangerous job. We often discussed together whether my husband should refuse to go to Belfast or other situations of danger for our son's sake, but this proved impossible, as he had signed a contract that bound him to fulfill his duty.

Increasingly, I felt lonely and isolated, disliking myself for my insecurities and vulnerability, but we are what we are at any moment in time. Watching too many news stories about the *Troubles* on British TV was quickly turning into an addictive pattern and immeasurably accelerated my fears and worries about my husband's safety. I imagined the camera crew in the line of fire, doing their duty, filming violent clashes between police and demonstrators in Belfast.

I became more and more worked up and upset about the unpredictable aspects of expressions of hatred and anger. Our large, rented mock-Tudor house in Ealing, a smart suburb of West London, could not give me the homely feeling I so needed after having the baby. I missed the support and closeness of family and friends. Perhaps I had post-natal depression and didn't know it?

Luckily, I had one very good friend who phoned me regularly and cheered me up in times of loneliness. We had met for the first time in the London office of German TV and struck up an instant friendship. My friend, Gisela, is also a German national and is married to a truly British gentleman. As luck would have it, we became pregnant almost at the same time and her first daughter was born only two weeks before my son's arrival. Gisela had worked in London for many years and lived with her family in South London. She became an important pillar in my life and a friend who would later walk on a similar spiritual path to me.

My son was about one year old when I noticed some changes in my husband's behavior, like, coming home extremely late at night and pretending to have to work at weekends. It took some time for him to admit that he was sharing his *time out* with another woman. Strangely enough, her name was also Louise. He suggested that we try to patch things up by living together like a modern couple in a so-called *open relationship*, giving each other permission to have extra-marital affairs. I often wondered if this *free-love-phenomenon* was the result of post-war upbringing?

Not such a happy family photograph,
shortly before the divorce

However, I certainly wasn't ready for such a life and found the entire idea incomprehensible, stressful and devoid of love. All I wanted to do is be a wife and mother and live happily ever after. This was not meant to be. Filming the political developments in Rhodesia, my husband met yet another woman, but she was determined to keep him. On his return to our family home, the future looked bleak and unhappy. Our marriage was failing rapidly.

To be honest, I still feel dizzy when I think about this time of my life. Everything collapsed. My body wasted down two dress

Encounter Between Two Worlds

sizes from a size 12 and I was considered to be quite skinny for my height of 5'7", or 172cm. I had to find a new home and a new job, as I could no longer work in the same office as my husband. Thankfully, I found work at Italian television at their London office, with one of the most popular and eccentric Italian TV personalities, a true, and I believe quite typical Sicilian. He had little sympathy for my role as a mother and I was often late from work picking up my son from a posh and expensive day nursery. Every morning, my son and I would ride there together on my rusty, noisy, secondhand moped from Fulham Road to Knightsbridge, my son tightly wrapped up in a warm blanket on the back seat.

Boris and me on my moped

I found some humor in this situation, as chauffeur-driven Bentleys and Rolls Royce's would drop off most of the other children. My strange presence in this smart environment did not go unnoticed, but countless eyes were diplomatically avoiding acknowledgment of our noisy arrival. For my son, this was a terrible time and he remembers to this day being very unhappy and unsettled.

My body batteries flashed a steady warning light, asking me to slow down and take care of myself, but how? I was the sole provider for my son and myself and I had to find a way to carry on. For a while I thought that I was struck down with some terrible illness, as all the parts of my body, both inside and outside, felt aching and troubled. My doctor gave me a prescription for tranquilizers and anti-depressants to calm my nerves. Thankfully, instead of following the doctor's recommended course of medication, I chose to join the *British Wheel of Yoga*.

I changed my diet, I became a vegetarian, and I changed my attitude to life. Eventually I felt stronger, healthier and more able to cope with my challenges.

The reader may wish to ask the question: *Why did you not leave England and go back home to have an easier life?* The answer is simple:

Firstly, I felt deeply ashamed about the breakup of my marriage, and although I wasn't the one who started stepping outside marital boundaries, I blamed myself. My mental and emotional programming was turned upside down, as I firmly believed that my marriage was for life. I was in a state of shock.

Secondly, I lost the person I considered to be my best and oldest friend in Germany. She, a good Catholic, dropped me like a hot potato when I told her that I was to be divorced, as this did not fit into her Christian beliefs.

Thirdly, I felt at odds with Germany and being German.

Fourthly, I was hoping to find something in England I feared I would not find in Germany:

I wanted to find myself.

On this journey to finding myself I took another wholesome step in the right direction. I became part of *The Yoga Ballet,* a group of twelve women, creating sketches of flowing Yoga movements to the sound of music. We performed publicly at the *Festival of Mind, Body and Spirit,* the Commonwealth Institute and many other venues.

Alexandra Palace, London, Yoga Event - Louise on right

Every Sunday morning I practiced together with the other lady yoginis in a center in Kensington. Our children would be taught in a separate class during this time and to my delight, my little boy turned out to be a *secret Yogi*. Although he could never be tempted to participate in class, being a shy boy with a preference to observe, he stood on his head and practiced everything he had seen the moment we returned home. Gradually, with the help of Yoga and the purposeful companionships arising from my interest in all things spiritual, my confidence and joy in life returned.

My son grew up completely bilingually. He learned stories, songs and nursery rhymes in both the English and German language without great effort. I could not have imagined the problems he would have to face after entering primary school. Some of the children started bullying him after finding out that he was German, calling him *little Hitler* and demonstrating in front of him the stereotypical German cartoon characters they had seen in their comics and magazines.

For a while my son was quite traumatized by all these experiences, but soon he found his own way of coping with the problem. He proclaimed that he was British through and through, as he was born in London, and he never spoke another word of German with me until he decided, at the age of twelve, to take German as a subject in school. As far as Boris was concerned, he was British. The fact that both of his parents were German made no difference to him, he was born in London and therefore, he was British. I had to respect his feelings, and our habit of conversing in the English language only with each other has persisted to the present day. Speaking German was totally reserved for his German grandmother, for oral examinations in German at school or if there was no other way of communicating with someone, like a non-English speaking relative.

Life goes on and every problem fades into the background at some point. However, certain elements or problems in one's life experience are not likely to fade away until the lessons are learned.

Perhaps my attitude to love was dominated by archetypal Libran characteristics? But perhaps lots of people are programmed to feel that they are only half a person without a partner to love at their side? I don't know, but the sense of equilibrium in my life very much depended on being in a loving relationship. I always imagined that *the other half* could give me what I thought was lacking in me, namely self-love, self-worth and a sense of wholeness. Not to forget another very important factor, I desperately wanted a father figure for my son, as his real father had meanwhile moved far away, to the other side of the world.

Sadly, I was lacking in the ability to read warning signs in problematic character traits in a man and my failed attempts to have a relationship with anyone else had a negative effect on my confidence. Ultimately, I was to try and fix all those confusing aspects of my character by studying the law of cause and effect in my own life, taking responsibility for myself and attending countless weird and wonderful alternative and New Age workshops.

The ability to love others
depends entirely on the ability
to love ourselves

(Anon)

Meeting M

In one of my soul-searching workshops I attracted the attention of a tall, dark and handsome stranger. I will call him M. My instincts and inner voice actually warned me against him, as I observed him flaunting his charm with the other female participants quite liberally. To my own surprise, all my alarm bells were soon switched off, my instincts successfully over-ruled. His French charm began to wear down my defenses, as he was quite different from anyone else I knew. Our mutual interest in the New Age movement appeared to me a good enough reason to believe that we could have a successful relationship. And, for a while, it seemed that happiness was a possibility.

M turned out to be a crazy and entertaining friend for my son. He did not take on the responsibilities of a father, not even temporarily, but he made my son laugh, taught him how to cook simple dishes, to fearlessly use herbs and spices, and he generally dared him to do things which I would have never allowed him to do, like letting him drive his relatively new BMW through the back streets of our London suburb. Boris was only 12, but the child in M matched the child in my son. Was this the appropriate male influence I was looking for?

One major problem started to emerge in our relationship. Not at first between M and myself, but between him and his parents. M was Jewish and the only son of a wealthy French businessman.

M had two sisters, one unmarried, the other divorced, who totally depended on M with regard to solving and surviving family problems and liaising with their parents. I was told that this was a son's duty in Jewish families, even though he was the youngest sibling.

When M confessed his love and relationship with me, a German woman, over the phone to his parents, he was instantly summoned to France. After his return, something had dramatically changed. His behavior towards me was without any warmth; there was now an icy and cynical air around us. M's father, whom he loved very much, had threatened to disinherit him, should he choose to stay with me.

This was all too much for me to handle. I signed up for a number of popular self-help workshops in London, to find answers to my dilemma:

Psychosynthesis, a branch of psychoanalysis founded by the Italian Roberto Assagioli. Also called a *transpersonal approach* because it integrates the spiritual aspect of human experience.

Rebirthing-Breathwork, a circular breathing technique which can help to overcome the *trauma* of being born and also release other traumas stored in the body on a cellular level; the founder was Leonard Orr.

EST Training. For those who have never heard about EST (Erhard Seminar Training, founded by the American author and lecturer Werner Erhard), I would like to give a brief explanation. In my opinion, these seminars were deliberately operated like military boot camps, without the physical aspect, like having to do one hundred push-ups, for example. We all volunteered to do mental and emotional push-ups in a smart hotel conference room, from early morning to early morning the next day, over a period of two and a half days, with dangerously restricted toilet breaks, to empower our self-discipline. The entire concept of these seminars was to break down our flawed existing mental and emotional structures and to start afresh after a weekend of tears, crisis, being bullied to the extreme, called names too rude to mention by the seminar leaders, feeling close to breakdown (and, some people did just that, they broke down and could not pull themselves up again). They prematurely had to leave the seminar, sadly missing out on countless rounds of mental missiles being fired in the direction of the participants, about 350 of us.

Up to that point in my life, I had always been very proud of my smiling, friendly nature, but one of the EST seminar trainers did not consider the ability to smile to be a virtue. He singled me out while standing in a straight line-up on top of the front stage with about twenty others, to be stared at by the rest of the participants and shouted, "Wipe that smirky smile of your face. You've been covering up your pain with that smile all your life. Get rid of it and be honest with yourself. Find out what's behind that friendly façade".

He quickly walked on to his next victim while I stood there, frozen to the spot, and then slowly falling apart. Have I ever felt so lonely, so vulnerable? A thousand daggers pierced my body and tears cascaded down my face. Sounds awful? **Yes it was**, but actively taking part in the re-structuring of Louise seemed a good idea at the time as I was thoroughly fed-up with who I was.

To counterbalance the severity and seriousness of my recent experiences, I signed up for a clowning workshop with the Actors Institute in London, expecting a weekend full of laughter and fun. Never did I imagine that it could be so hard to make people laugh. *How do professional clowns do it? Are they naturally funny people or can clowning be learned?* I soon found out that my biggest obstacle was the fact that I could not take myself lightly, could not drop my fear of looking ridiculous and of being unable to make anyone laugh, at least this was my problem on the first day of the workshop.

According to a British belief, there was no such thing as a *funny German*. I often heard this being said at the time, even on television, *The Germans have no sense of humor*. With this programming in mind, I painfully and ridiculously inhibited myself. Can I jump this hurdle? Could I prove them all wrong and be the first German to make them laugh? What a tall order. I had one more day to conquer my fears and to express the funny side of my character. The second day of the workshop had to be different. I did not want to go home feeling a total failure and had made up my mind that I would let go of my inhibitions, let go of *fearful Louise*. It worked. I can't remember what I did to make the others laugh, but what I do know is that it came from deep within, from a place of fearlessness. I painted my face, found a funny story somewhere inside of me, thoroughly enjoyed performing and then relished the happy smiles and laughter of the other eleven participants as a response to my efforts. This was a major breakthrough. After careful analysis of this happening I came to the conclusion that it was a miracle.

It is hard to pinpoint the overall effect of any of these courses I had participated in, but somehow, my inner core felt strengthened. They all contributed in their different ways to me, to finding myself. My determination to heal myself from whatever it was that was creating so much pain in my life grew stronger and stronger.

It may seem self-indulgent to some, but I believe that we owe it to ourselves to find out who we are. This is possibly the very reason for our existence.

Dating back to about 1400 BC, the ancient Greeks consulted the Oracle of Delphi to find answers to their questions. The Oracle states*: Know Thyself.... Learn how to be who you are.*

The Indian Holy Man Sai Baba (whom I visit a few years later) pointed out that *we are three people: The one other people think we are. The one we think we are. And the one we truly are.* Who are we truly and how can we find out? Another saying of his that stuck in my mind was: *We are not human beings trying to have a divine experience, but we are divine beings having a human experience.*

Somehow, all of this was beginning to make sense to me. In order to make my human experience a divine one, I tried to strip away the clutter of my conditioning and fearlessly take off layer by layer.

Feeling less inhibited and more in tune with my talents, I joined the Streatham Operatic Society. My love of music and singing could be expressed in a, for me, perfect combination. Little did I know that the society was preparing for a commemorative show, celebrating 50 years of bringing operatic joy to a faithful audience.

Of course wartime songs played a large role when it came to choosing the material to be performed. I learned songs like *Keep the Home Fires Burning*, *The White Cliffs of Dover* and...*Lili Marlene*, a song made famous by Marlene Dietrich. I should not have been surprised to hear that I was the natural choice to sing *Lili Marlene* in German – solo.

My mind conjured up visions of being stoned on stage (yes, I know I'm a drama queen), or at least covered with rotten tomatoes, thrown at me by a furious crowd. This fear had to be mentioned to my operatic colleagues.

They laughed out loud and told me that my problem was nothing that a stiff drink wouldn't cure. And that was the end of it!

Singing *Lili Marlene* became another positive milestone in my search for myself, and overcoming my fears about being German.

This is my step-by-step guide to becoming *Lili*:

I built my own lamp post, asked my mother if she had some wartime glittery clothes hidden away somewhere, bought a beret, learned the lyrics and tune and tried to copy and sing the song with the same husky voice as Marlene Dietrich.

The opening night and performing the song on stage had aroused great excitement in me, more than I could have ever imagined.

Louise singing 'Lili Marlene' for
Streatham Operatics - London

Performance night: the school hall slowly filled with people who demonstrated their love for everything we did, for every song we sang, with wild clapping, foot stamping and whistles. I could sense strong emotions in the hall, especially amongst the elderly. But when *Lili Marlene* slowly walked across the stage with her lamppost and sang her heart out to all the invisible soldiers, I could hear a medley of sounds reverberating throughout the hall, tissues being pulled from handbags and pockets, tears being wiped and lots of gentle sniffles. To further heighten the impact of the song it had been decided that the entire choir would continue with the English lyrics, after the original German version had been sung by me. It sounded beautiful, heartwarming, right out of a movie. At its conclusion, there was a brief pause, a silence and then…rapture and huge applause. What a success!

After the show, I went home with a glad and happy heart, still humming '*Vor der Kaserne, vor dem grossen Tor…wie einst Lili Marlene'*, in English, *'Underneath the lantern, by the barracks gate…Like then, Lili Marlene'*.

I could sense that I had made considerable progress. This progress was measured by how others, especially Jewish people, responded to me, after finding out that I was German. I no longer pretended that I was someone else and stopped creating a total mystery around my background. I took the *risk* to be honest about me and about my nationality.

M was still in my life, from time to time, but before we parted for good, he told me about his father's true reason for hating all Germans:

During the war, the Nazis had killed his father's beloved older brother, who had acted like a father figure for most of his teenage life and with whom he had a very close bond. This left him heartbroken and very angry. He could not forgive this cruel act and held it against all Germans, including me.

Knowing this helped me understand the dynamics and difficulties arising for the entire family from our relationship, but sadly, forgiveness was not an option for M's parents. Did the fact that I finally knew why I was not acceptable as a partner for M lessen my heartache? No, not really, but at least it helped me to feel more compassionate about M's dilemma and I could forgive him for the way he handled our relationship.

The drama of being born a German had extended into my love life and somehow, that made it even worse. Why did I still have to go through this, after all my hard work and efforts to break free?

I thought that I had cracked the code, broken the pattern. I remembered something I had learned in the Psychosynthesis workshops, the metaphor of the *spiral* or *ladder*. We only think that we are still stuck at the same place, experiencing the same old thing again and again, but in fact, we have moved to another level of consciousness. The experience seems the same, but it is experienced from another standpoint. The famous symbolism of *peeling away the layers of an onion* comes to mind too, or of *a snake leaving its old skin behind* and starting life all over again in a new skin.

9

Another Emotional Dilemma

How could I change my experience of the world, of life, for good? Where was I on the *ladder* for success? How close was I to breaking old patterns, which did not serve me? How many layers had I already peeled off to start on the road to a happier life? And how many more layers are there?

Time and time again, this one sentence was repeated in every workshop I attended: ***We create our own universe.*** If this is the case, *I am rubbish at it,* I thought, *totally lacking in the ability to create a pleasant universe for myself.* Was I truly addicted to suffering? Is there such a thing as an addiction to suffering? Why was being a German such a problem for me? Did other Germans feel the same way as I did and share my experience or similar experiences? I would love to find out, but I never dared to ask anyone this question, thinking that I was possibly the one causing my own trauma.

I needed to constructively do something else to get more answers to my endless stream of questions and signed up for a counseling course. The course was scheduled to run over three months and consisted of several lectures with all participants present, about 200 people, followed by splitting the large group into small practice and observation therapy groups. All was well, until our therapy sessions were focused on us, the participants and not as in previous meetings, on potential clients. We all shared our innermost feelings and concerns with each other, being directed and supported by one of the designated group leaders. I always believed that their role was to create a safe space for all participants in which they can open up and turn themselves inside out. In one of the sessions, I felt overcome by the need to share my feelings about my German/Jewish conflict and the loss of my relationship with M.

Emotions overcame me and I ended up in floods of tears, and so did the other group members who were listening to my story. Only one woman sitting opposite me had a different emotion. She looked angrily at me and informed me that she was Jewish. My heart sank and I started once again to apologize for who I was and on behalf of the German nation. Again, nothing I could say was of any consequence. The woman was as angry with me, as she was with all Germans. She was also angry with the rest of the group for daring to feel sympathy for me. She told the others that if they wanted to feel sorry for anyone, it should be for her. In her eyes, I had no right as a German to even voice my difficulties and problems and worst of all, to get sympathy from others. To my great shock, our group leader confirmed this and told me with a firm voice that I had to give consideration to what I had just heard. After all, I was the perpetrator and she was the victim. Perpetrator??? Victim??? That kind of rhetoric was new to me, and his words hit me like a rock.

There was no understanding for my heartache and the personal crisis I had shared with the group. No mention that this was a counseling course and not a war tribunal and that I had every right to express my feelings, just like everyone else. Or had I? My safe space was pulled away from under my feet.

What would you, the reader, have to say to me in such circumstances?

I drove home in a sea of tears. Devastated. Betrayed. My trust in our counseling group had vanished. What occurred on that evening made me feel as if I had no right to express my emotions, just because…I was born a German?

This is not an over-dramatized version of the truth, but exactly how I experienced and felt about the unfolding events at the time.

I am now able to write the story down without attachment to it, but of course during that period, I was in pain.

Will I ever be able to shake off this German stigma? Is it essential for me as an individual, in order to find inner peace, self-respect and self-love, to come to terms with and to fully understand the awful crimes committed by some people in the country of my birth, before I was even born? Where does my responsibility lie? Have I the right to be free of the burden of such crimes? Questions tormented me and found no permanent solutions.

Human resilience is a remarkable built-in attribute. I know now that there must be moments in everyone's life, which are so painful and desperate that it is hard to see the light at the end of the tunnel. But miraculously, for those of us who survive the crisis, there is always a brighter day on the horizon.

10

Hardworking Woman

Getting on with life and my career as a freelance film editor, I was suddenly immersed in regular work for one particular channel of German Television. Looking back it feels as if I worked 24/7 in this job. My private life shrank to a minimum as our small team was always on standby to rush to the office and produce urgent news items in times of crisis. I loved my work when there was no crisis, no bombs, no dead bodies, and no political panic. I enjoyed creating stories about the UK's rich cultural heritage, the arts, theatre, musical events and yes, I admit it, I always loved to produce stories about the Royal Family, especially Royal weddings. Germans have a soft spot for… no, a real obsession with the British Royal Family. I am not sure that the British public are aware of this obsession, love, affection and curiosity. Even an incident like a fishbone stuck in the Queen Mother's throat, or her need for a hip replacement was of great importance to the German media and it would be turned into an endless stream of news stories. Did she know that we Germans loved her so much and cared for her wellbeing? I don't think so, as the Queen Mother for her part disliked the Germans and blamed them for the early death of her beloved husband, King George V. Nevertheless, German Television cared, and the tireless efforts of many of the Royal Family to fulfill their public duties, kept us all busy and happy in between points of crisis.

Although my job was at times exciting, fulfilling and privileged, I do not wish to spend much time thinking about this part of my life, as I sometimes feel a deep regret and pain about the lack of time I had for my son. But what were my alternatives? In order to keep my job, I had to show commitment and be prepared to work at all times, even at weekends.

My ex-husband had meanwhile remarried, started a new family and lived in a faraway country, away from his obligations as a father and beyond the legal jurisdiction of the UK and Germany. Without receiving any financial help from him, I had to work to support our little family.

Later in life, after expressing my deep regrets to my son about how our life had turned out and how I wished that I'd been around more to watch him grow up, he reassured me that he thought that I had done my best to look after him. Somehow, although I appreciated his kind and consoling words, for me it is a different story. I would love to turn back the clock, just to spend more time with him when he was growing up!

There I was, a hardworking woman, and the news kept coming in, relentlessly. *Good news is bad news for television* our London correspondent, my boss, used to say. There was hardly any good news for a very long time. A whole series of tragedies and disasters struck Britain during the 1980s:

> March 1987 - the tragic Zeebrugge Ferry disaster in the North Sea – 193 people dead,
>
> November 1987 - the King's Cross London Underground fire – 31 people dead,
>
> early December 1988 - rail accident on Britain's busiest rail junction, Clapham Junction, London – 35 dead,
>
> December 1988, a terrorist bomb on a plane heading for America - blowing up above Lockerbie,

Scotland, killing 259 passengers and 11 people on the ground,

January 1989 - the Kegworth air disaster on the M1 - 46 people dead,

April 1989 - the Hillsborough football disaster, where 96 people were literally pushed to their death behind a security barrier, right in front of the TV cameras.

I am not even counting the many other dramas or all the other stories related to life in the UK, which also kept us busy in between the major ones, but the Hillsborough disaster was for me *the straw that broke the camel's back*. The relentless confrontation with human drama had burned me out.

My body had begun to feel the effect of my work, having to cover so many tragic events. People forget that on television they see only a fraction of what is really happening. The presenter, journalist, camera or sound person and the film editor often have to watch the most horrendous images again and again, before editing them into a palatable news item, safe enough to be watched by children, pregnant women and elderly people. My body was giving in. I could no longer sleep well, my heart started to have unpleasant palpitations, and tears were just below the surface. Emotionally, I walked on a knife's edge and could not take any more. The constant bombardment of human misery and extreme emotional pain was becoming too much to bear. My male colleagues all seemed to be able to deal with it a lot better. We had endless discussions in the office about our role as compassionate human beings versus being a professional at work, especially after the Hillsborough disaster.

Apparently, 41 lives, out of the 96 who died, had the potential to survive.

I had the view that members of the media who were present, should drop their cameras, notebooks, sound gear etc. and give a helping hand for the rescue of people. Some of my male colleagues, however, thought that it was the media's job to produce a historic record and therefore keep on working, regardless or because of the unfolding drama. The debate turned into an argument. In the end my colleagues thought that I was oversensitive, possibly overworked, and therefore not able to get my priorities right.

Again I ask you, the reader: *What would you do? What is the right response?*

One image that persistently kept coming up in my mind was that of television viewers, sitting at home with their feet up to relax, a nice drink, a cool beer or mug of tea, salted peanuts, crisps and lots of nibbles, hot slices of pizza, while those producing the news programs often endure extreme stress to deliver the product on time. Contributing to my personal dilemma was the fact that I was not part of a British trade union. I was not protected from unreasonable working hours, nor was I part of the German system, as I had an English contract with a German company, a rather complex and unsettling feature. Basically, to keep my job, I had to work all hours, whenever the need.

Some of my colleagues had already suffered heart attacks or showed other physical and mental symptoms, due to work-related stress. It was quite clear to me, that I very much deserved a break and some time out.

Concerned for my health, I decided to visit my doctor. I described my symptoms to the relatively unconcerned doctor, and ended up with a prescription for tranquilizers. Leaving the surgery, I tore the paper into small pieces. *No, this is not the right path for me*, I thought, *I have to change my life dramatically.*

I felt compelled to look for an alternative method of healing, a method which would truly *heal* me and not merely suppress my symptoms. For quite some time I had been curious about the possibility of evoking our self-healing-power by the laying on of hands. Could that be a solution? Finding out the phone number of the National Federation of Spiritual Healers was no problem and I enquired about healers in my area. To my great relief, I was able to make an appointment straightaway, as the healing clinic in Croydon, near to where I was living at the time, was open and running for the next few hours. *Take charge*, I commanded myself, *your health is important.*

I called work and said that I would be late. This was something I had never done before. My family and teachers raised me with an extreme work ethic and commitment to work and employers, but this time I had to look after myself. I didn't even feel guilty, and that was a major step forward.

Life isn't about
waiting for the storm
to pass,
it's about learning to dance
in the rain

(Anon)

Healing Journey

I believe that the right person or healing method always comes along at the right time. At least for me, this was and still is my experience. I called out for help and did not have to wait long for a major pointer in the right direction. I am a firm believer in there being a larger spiritual family in which the various members pop up throughout our life and we give love and support to each other in many ways.

I felt excited and anxious at the same time, as I had never experienced the laying on of hands and the potential for healing arising from that. The large hall in Croydon was packed with people in need of help. I guess that many of them must have felt the same inner calling as I did to come to this place. I had time to observe, inhale and bathe in this incredible, tangible energy of healing love and peace. Whatever was happening here was happening quietly. Healers in white coats stood or sat silently with their clients, slowly moving their hands over those areas in need of healing. I was mesmerized. Work and all of my problems seemed light years away. This scene in front of my eyes could have been a set-up for a painting. I would give the artwork the name: *Serenity in a freeze frame* or *Silence please – Angels at work*. Time stood still.

Yes, I was definitely in the right place. But there was more. I had a sensation of *homecoming* and *familiarity*.

My turn. I walked over to the healer and was greeted with a warm smile. Had we met before? My healer was a kindly looking woman called Bettine. She and her husband had been doing this kind of work for many years and were totally committed to helping others. It was through the sudden and unfortunate loss of one of their daughters that both were guided to start a spiritual healing clinic.

Many questions were asked before my treatment could begin. My tears were abundant. The nightmare of all the things I'd seen in the past few months and then turned into news stories was sticking like a layer of tar to my heart. During this single session with my healer I experienced a huge release of emotional pain. Before my healing session I felt as if I'd carried the world on my shoulders and all of its problems in my heart; afterwards, the world carried itself, at least for a while. What a relief!

Bettine gave me a big hug and I floated towards the railway station and back to work.

My next appointment was for the following week, but this time it was to be in her home in the evening.

London Victoria to Croydon train on time, it said on the notice board. Bless British Rail; for once the train was on time, a very rare occurrence, and, on that day, a very welcome one indeed.

I was excited about my appointment and about having a healing session in the comfort of Bettine's home. Curiosity got the better of me, as I was keen to find out how this unusual couple lived and why they opened their home in the evening to help so many desperate people. The house door was left on the latch, so that visitors could quietly enter, take a seat in the hallway and wait for their turn. Greeted by the soothing and relaxing sound of music, I felt immediately at home and very welcome. This place was indeed a healing sanctuary. With eyes closed, I waited for my turn, feeling at peace, happy and expectant. Both treatment rooms were still busy with other clients.

Suddenly, a soft murmur and Bettine's door opened. She had a big, warm and motherly smile on her face, motioned *Goodbye* to her previous client who looked fairly blissed out, and then put her arms around me for a heartfelt hug. We sat down to talk about the latest events in my life and any aches and pains I was experiencing in my body. There was a distinct serenity and calm surrounding us. The room was pretty and simply furnished, two chairs, a little table, flowers, an image of Christ and...who was he? For a brief moment I was spellbound, as I looked into the most mysterious dark eyes I had ever seen. Why did the image of someone's eyes have such an impact on me?

I had my eyes closed while the healer *tuned in*, and relaxed so much that I briefly nodded off. When I emerged from slumber, Bettine had already begun with her calming healing procedure. I felt so light, as if angel's wings had been gently stroking me. Tears of gratitude streamed down my cheeks. Oh, it was high time I found my way here.

Constant stress had eaten its way into my mind and body. Right now, I just felt happy that I had been strong enough to swap the medical prescription for tranquilizers for a much healthier alternative. Bettine handed me tissues from a big box. Obviously, I was not the only one shedding tears here. It felt so good to cry in this supportive space, so safe to release the tension, which had built up in my body.

To my surprise there was no charge for this wonderful healing service. A small box indicated that a donation would be welcome and could be made at one's discretion and financial ability to help the continuation of this work.

On getting up from my chair I noticed *the eyes* again.

"Who is he?" I heard myself asking.

"Oh, he is our guru, Sai Baba, a Holy Man and Avatar (in the Hindu tradition, an Avatar is believed to be an incarnation of a deity) who lives in Southern India. We have lots of books about him in our library. Are you interested?"

Sure I was interested. Long before the Beatles discovered their Maharishi Mahesh Yogi, when I was only a young girl, I knew that one day I would go to India; that was my greatest wish. Was Sai Baba the reason I had to go?

Life is a Game, Play It, by Joy Thomas, was to be my first book.

I took it home like a treasure that I had found at the bottom of the ocean. That night was reading night. My first reaction to what I was reading did not have the expected outcome. I felt annoyed.

What a load of sticky sweet exaggerated nonsense, I thought. *How can Joy Thomas, how can anyone be taken in by a living guru? He is only a man, living, breathing, walking the Earth just like we do. How could he be so special? People say that he is a miracle man and miracles only happened two thousand years ago when Jesus was alive, or in Hollywood movies. He doesn't even look like a guru, they usually have long grey hair and a beard and smile serenely to get our attention.*

The most off-putting aspect was that this guru claimed to be *God on Earth,* but then he went on to say that *we are also God.* The only difference, he said, between him and us is that we don't know it, we are not conscious of our divinity. He is suggesting that each one of us is a co-creator of the Universe. Now, that's a bit strong, isn't it?

What I imagined might bring me great happiness and a new opening, spiritually, physically and mentally, seemed to burst like a bubble, but only momentarily. I realized that my fickle and judgmental approach to Joy Thomas' book, or anything unknown and strange to me for that matter, didn't get me any further. Frustrated with myself I kept on reading. The mere fact that I had never experienced a living guru and whatever we call miracles, nor heard about any of the concepts and teachings he stands for, gave me no right to be so condemning. What would I think about a person who outright dismisses something or someone, without giving them the benefit of the doubt? *Stay open-minded,* I told myself. Perhaps another book would be more appealing to me and bring me closer to the truth.

My next attempt to achieve this was to read *Sai Baba: A Man of Miracles,* written by an Australian author, Howard Murphet, who was quite an intriguing character, I found out. He was born in Tasmania in 1906 and educated at the University of Hobart. Obviously, a down-to-earth man with experiences of serving in the British Eighth Army in the war at El Alamein and Tunis, taking part in the invasion of Sicily and Italy and later of

Normandy. He was also in charge of the British Press Section at the Nuremberg Trials. He visited India in 1964 to study Yoga and Eastern philosophy. It was then that he came across Sai Baba, whom he visited in 1966, experiencing miracle after miracle.

I read about Howard's spiritual journey with fascination and great excitement. Here I had another style of writing, another incredible journey of discovery, but equally as unbelievable as the book by Joy Thomas. What is this sticky sweet love people experience and describe at great length? It is not human love, it seems. Could we possibly be capable of finding a love much greater than our love for others, for family and friends? Experience and statistics sadly show us that this human love can often evaporate like a water puddle in the desert sun. Is it the role of a guru, or any spiritual teacher, to guide us into a much more expansive, greater, deeper, eternal love zone? And is this great love felt like sweetness and bliss by all who are privileged to experience it?

What on earth happens to all those who have an encounter with this Holy Man? People are literally bowled over and turned into pink marshmallows. The experience is apparently life changing, miraculous, but certainly not always easy. I then read, no, devoured, several other books by different authors, Dr. Samuel Sandweiss, Peggy Mason, Ron Laing…all ringing the same heavenly bells of glory for this far-away being in an orange robe. I had to check him out, give him the benefit of the doubt.

This was my personal call to go to India.

When you think that you have reached
the darkest place inside yourself –
Search for the light that guides you.
Grasp it - and hold on to it!

L. I-M

12

The Story of Al Drucker

Now that I'd made up my mind to go and see a Holy Man in India, everything was going my way. Well almost. My newfound direction in life sparked a fair amount of controversy amongst some of my friends, relatives and acquaintances. Anger, hostility, resentment and ridicule were only some of the emotions expressed towards me. I was taken aback, surprised and pained, as I lost two of my oldest friends, just because... What on earth triggers such a response? Why was it so hard for some to accept my need to go on a spiritual quest? After all, I wasn't joining a cult or a sect; I merely wanted to visit a Holy Man. I would be very happy for anyone, if they found a way, a path, any path, as long as it is peaceful and doesn't harm self or others. On closer inspection I found out that it was the idea of visiting a guru that turned out to be the problem. But the word *guru* only means teacher, and sometimes, when we are stuck in a pattern which doesn't serve us, such a teacher, if he is wise and good, can guide us to find our way back to *ourselves*. That's all I want, find myself and leave some bad habits behind in the process. Nothing and nobody can stop me going to India!

I was able to convince my boss that I needed a four-week break from work. My healer put me in touch with a couple from North London, Sandra and Aime, who accompanied groups of spiritual seekers on a regular basis to the ashram in Southern

India where Sai Baba lived. They informed me that I had just missed a major gathering of *devotees* in Hamburg earlier that year, in 1990, which could have been a good preparation for going to India. The good news was that help was at hand. Aime posted me an audiocassette recorded at the Hamburg meeting, with devotional songs and all the key speeches. I instantly created a space to listen them.

All such gatherings start with devotional songs, called *Bhajans*. The magical sound of Indian instruments, the unusual beat, songs in Hindi and Sanskrit, it all sounded totally new to me, but not foreign. I let myself be carried away and uplifted by the tablas (Indian drums), an Indian harmonium, and powerful singing voices. The devotional songs on the audiocassette concluded with *OM – Shanti–Shanti–Shanti, OM – Peace-Peace-Peace*. Then the main guest speaker was announced, his name, Al Drucker. He had come all the way from America to Hamburg to speak about his personal experiences with his guru. He said that he had previously worked as a nuclear physicist on ballistic missile programs and nuclear weapons for the American Armed Forces. He knew that this was not the way he wanted to spend his life. His body caved in under the stress and he ultimately suffered from severe stomach ulcers, forcing him to spend a lot of time in hospitals for treatment.

Disillusioned with his job, Al went on a major journey of self-discovery to India. After a lengthy search in 1974, he finally found what he was looking for in a tiny village called Puttaparthi, in the South Indian state of Andhra Pradesh where Sai Baba's ashram had been established.

Al's story sent chills down my spine. This is his story:

Al was born a German Jew. In the late 1930s, when he was only 9 years old, his parents had put him on a train from Berlin to Poland. They had bought him a 1st class ticket, although Jewish people at that time were not allowed to travel 1st class. The train stopped in Potsdam. A German soldier opened the door, shouted *Heil Hitler* and saluted the SS officer (State Security) behind him, to be greeted with the same salute in return. The officer was dressed in black, skull on hat, black belt, boots, gloves, gun, and swastika on jacket.

The officer entered the train compartment where Al was sitting, motioned the soldier to go away and closed the door behind him. Al was terrified and jumped up from his seat, only to be told "Sit down".

The little boy was frightened. Then the officer sat down and made himself comfortable, took off his belt, boots, hat, gloves, jacket, and loosened his collar.

"Do you know any Bible stories?" he asked the boy, knowing very well that Al was Jewish, as a German boy of his age would not have been travelling without wearing the appropriate Hitler Youth uniform. Not quite knowing how to respond to the officer, Al said, "No, I don't know any Bible stories".

"I will tell you some", the officer replied. For two hours he sat with the boy, telling him stories from the Old Testament about Moses, Daniel, Joseph and Esther. He obviously knew his Bible well and presented the stories insightfully and with charm. Al had lost all fear.

Finally the officer said, "Come close, I must tell you something. This country has gone crazy. It has gone insane. There will be a lot of trouble and you are going in the wrong direction by travelling to Poland. Go back home and tell your parents that you should all leave Germany and go west".

The train stopped. The officer dressed himself and the soldier opened the door for him. *Heil Hitler* was exchanged again, heels speedily clicked against each other. The officer looked back at the boy with a benevolent smile, closed the door and left. Al's last impression was the SS emblem on his jacket.

Al stayed only briefly in Poland. On his return home, he told his parents about meeting the SS officer and urged them to leave Germany as soon as possible and go west. Despite many obstacles, the family was able to obtain their exit visas and flee the country in time.

Many years later, in a personal interview with Sai Baba, he asked Al out of the blue "Do you remember the SS officer in the train when you were a little boy? That was me. I told you to leave Germany".

Al was stunned. How could he have known about this very personal incident from so many years ago? It had always been a private family story. In fact, he was so impressed with Sai Baba that he ended up living in the tiny village of Puttaparthi, teaching science for many years at the Holy Man's renowned University.

Can I actually grasp and understand what I had just heard? Here we have a nuclear scientist talking absolutely clearly, and as a matter of fact, about an event which saved his family in the most extraordinary way. And then he meets a guru, forty-something years later, telling Al that it was he who rescued him. What a story! But how could Sai Baba know about such a personal event in Al's life? How could he claim that he had been the SS officer? Who in their right mind would admit to being such a person, and if they did, what could possibly be the reason behind it? I figured that it was perhaps the only safe disguise to adopt in order to be able to communicate with a Jewish boy under the circumstances.

In the past I had read about *unusually gifted people* who seem to have the ability to be in more than one place at the same time. One of these extraordinary people was the well-known Catholic priest, stigmatist and mystic Padre Pio, also known as Saint Pio of Pietrelcina, Italy, who lived amongst us until 1968. He, like Sai Baba, was known to have appeared in two locations simultaneously (bi-location phenomena), even outside his home country, Italy. I would like to elaborate on one story that impressed me:

During World War II, an order to bomb the area of San Giovanni Rotondo, Italy, was given to American and English pilots. Flying above their target, they were getting ready to drop their bombs, but something extraordinary stopped them from doing so. After their return to base, all of them reported seeing a priest in the air, stretching out his hands with the signs of stigmata on them, preventing the pilots from dropping their bombs.

This is just one of many stories about this remarkable Saint, but I am wondering if Sai Baba is also one of these *special people*? Can he be in India and somewhere else simultaneously; in a different body and an different set of clothing, or does he communicate his message through a chosen being? Does he know things about me? I had more questions than answers in my head.

A strong desire to meet Al welled up inside of me. I wanted to tell him that his speech had a huge impact and acted like a catalyst for my spiritual journey. And I wanted to tell him how grateful I was that he gave his speech in Hamburg, in front of a mainly German audience.

Some years later, in April 2000, I met Al Drucker at a Sai Baba event at a college in Hampshire, England. I had no idea what Al looked like, but shortly after my arrival I noticed a man walking determinedly towards our conference hall inside the college grounds. *This can only be Al Drucker*, I thought and made a beeline for him. Sure enough, my instinct did not betray me. He greeted me with a big smile and open arms. I told him that I had been waiting for ten years to make his acquaintance and how much the speech he gave in Hamburg in 1990 had changed my life.

While walking along, I continued to tell him about *my story* and how guilty I felt about being a German. He stopped in his tracks, moved his head forward towards mine, looked at me with great seriousness and penetrating eyes and said:

"**Let me tell you something, you are not the story. Tell the story, but do not feel attached to it, that only creates pain. I felt guilty all my life. All Jews feel guilty. All Germans feel guilty. All human beings feel guilty about one thing or another. We are all born with guilt. Always remember: You are not the story. Be happy**".

His insightful comment made me laugh with joy. Here I was with my big drama and he took the *wind out of my sails*, calmed me down at an instant, making guilt a general human condition, not just a German/Jewish one. I felt that I could trust in the truth of Al's insightful comment, as it was made not only from a Jewish perspective, but most likely from an objective perspective. I am forever grateful for this encounter, as a door had been opened for me to a completely new way of thinking about my problem with guilt. My German guilt had a *purpose*! Although I did not know at this stage of my life what this purpose was, I imagined it to be like a catapult sending me in the right direction to find myself.

See, I have set before you
Life and Death;
Therefore, choose Life.
The Torah

(From The Complete Jewish Bible by David H. Stern)

13

Two More Obstacles and Preparations for India

My trip to India was getting closer. I had to overcome only one more obstacle, I thought, my mother. She was shocked about my decision to see Sai Baba and very fearful, which resulted in many difficult discussions between us. My mother was frightened that I would be forced to stay in India, in what she imagined to be a cult, be stripped of all mental faculties and coerced into transferring every penny of my savings into my guru's bank account.

Despite the fact that I was forty years old and had lived an independent life for a great number of years, she begged my best friend, Gisela, to travel with me to India for my protection and to keep an eye on me. In my mother's opinion I was a dreamy and vulnerable sort of a person, but Gisela was level-headed, reliable and not easily fooled. I always knew that I also had these qualities, but my mother did sadly not recognize that. Funnily, my friend had absolutely no interest in spiritual teachers, but she was willing to read up on my chosen guru and report back to my mother about her findings.

Gisela *devoured* book after book about Sai Baba and could find nothing unacceptable in Sai Baba's teachings or the stories written by his devotees. On the contrary, she only found good common sense, compassion and love.

My dear mother felt comforted by the fact that nothing

disturbing could be found in any of the literature. It was agreed that my friend did not have to accompany me to India. If my mother was still worried about me, credit to her, she kept all her concerns to herself. I was finally free to plan for my journey.

A few weeks prior to the trip to India, the tour organizers, Sandra and Aime, had arranged a meeting for all the *pilgrims* in their lovely home in London. This was a customary procedure, as most groups were rather large and certain ground rules had to be established. Fifty people from the UK and Ireland had signed up to see Sai Baba for this visit, but not everybody was able to attend our gathering.

Sandra and Aime welcomed me like a long-lost member of their family. Did they not know that I was German? I could not help having this *here we go again* feeling. Why on earth did I feel like that? I had no logical explanation at hand and overruled my busy monkey-mind to enjoy the moment and my new-found friends who made me feel welcome and at home. The fact that I was the only German in the group did not seem to bother anyone.

The members of our group were a *colorful* bunch from various walks of life, aged between eighteen and almost eighty. What amazed me most was the fact that everybody had a story to tell as to how they had found out about Sai Baba. In the course of the afternoon we introduced ourselves and briefly shared our personal reasons for going to see him. Some of the stories were remarkable, impossible, positively outrageous and miraculous, awe-inspiring and would be extremely difficult to repeat in the company of skeptics.

Thank God that we live in times and in a country where we can express and communicate such stories, I thought, and felt very privileged to be part of this group of inspirational and warmhearted people.

One couple, Linda and Alan, had sold their home in order to finance their trip to India. She was a pretty woman in a wheelchair, and both she and her husband were hoping for a cure for her or at least for an interview with Sai Baba. He is apparently known to have cured countless people from all over the world of life-threatening and terminal illnesses, including cancer.

Encounter Between Two Worlds

There are plenty of books on the subject of his miracles, but it does not seem appropriate here to relay such *secondhand* stories. I have made an exception in the case of Al Drucker, as his story intertwines with mine.

Our group meeting left me feeling elated and confident in the knowledge that I was doing the right thing at the right time. The seeds of fear and doubt some people had tried to plant in my head, had not germinated. Soon, my dream would come true and I would find out why India had been calling me for so long. All that was left for me to do now was to go shopping and prepare for my life-changing adventure.

"Travel lightly", Sai Baba had said to a devotee whose book I read. I understood these two words to mean firstly *travel lightly through life, without too many attachments to worldly things* and secondly *to travel without burdening yourself with a heavy, cumbersome suitcase*. Those two words *travel lightly*, had made an impression, and I was determined to take them seriously. I will only travel with the absolute minimum. My shopping list made me smile:

> Lightweight rucksack
> Citronella aroma oil (to keep mosquitoes away)
> Clothes pegs
> Sterilizing tablets (to sterilize fruit and vegetables)
> Disinfectant liquid, large bottle
> Sachets of disinfectant wipes
> Insect repellent
> Punjabi suit (a pair of baggy trousers and a pretty tunic-like top from one of the many Indian shops in Tooting, London).

Happiness is a shopping list, which points you in a new direction of life!

This moment of happiness was to be challenged dramatically by news about the Gulf War, which started in August 1990, but culminated into a full-blown war on the 17th January 1991, two days prior to my trip to India. At the London office of German Television preparations were made to report about the war around the clock. All news programs had to be constantly fed with new footage from the warzone. My boss made it quite clear to me that I had to cancel my holiday immediately. There was no way I could leave work at this time, everybody was needed.

What was I to do now? My dream could burst like a bubble at an instant. I told my boss that I would give him an answer the next day, 18th January, and that I had to think carefully about making the right decision. A flash of annoyance passed over his face. It was pretty clear and obvious to him what choice I should make, but my head was spinning and I could not commit to saying to him there and then, that I would be staying in London, enduring and working through yet another traumatic and painful period of world history.

My train journey home turned into pure torment. I cried all the way from Victoria Station to Croydon. Some of my fellow-passengers gave me very compassionate looks; others appeared slightly irritated by my display of emotions.

Glad to be at home with my family and getting all the support and love I needed to make a decision that was right for me and nobody else, I retreated into my bedroom for a long prayer and meditation. Slowly my calm returned, emotions pushed to the side, and I could think more clearly. My inner voice literally begged me to be strong and stand up for myself. I knew in the depth of my heart and soul, that I did not want to produce news stories about the war for the coming week or even weeks, watching and editing films of wounded or dead soldiers being carried away, bombs exploding…the entire range of human drama and emotions unfolding. I had enough of it, couldn't do it any more. I had come to the end of my endurance, as I was possibly heading for burnout.

To be absolutely sure what my next step should be I decided to consult various divination devices, the I Ching, the Tarot and the Rune Stones. All of them pointed in the same direction, *Go, Louise, go! This is important for your soul journey.* The combination of Rune Stones that I had picked turned out to be particularly meaningful and encouraging. The stones simply informed me that the journey I was about to undertake was a matter of life and death. They implied that an essential death of *the old self* would occur and that nothing would ever be the same again. Not following my heart could result in a personal drama or crisis. Did I need to hear any more? Certainly not, I just had to go to India and live with the consequences, as far as work was concerned.

Next day, the office atmosphere was already charged with a frantic buzz when I arrived in the morning. Everyone was full throttle ahead in war mode. My heart started to pound when I climbed up the stairs to my boss's office. The door stood wide open, he sat at his desk reading the daily papers.

I have to say at this point that I had a good boss, whom I hugely respected for his professionalism and general nice-ness to all staff, and his human qualities were never in question. This was not a personal vendetta on my part, I had never let anybody down in the past, never neglected my work obligations, but I just had to go away, now, tomorrow, despite the looming disaster.

He knew what was coming, as he chose to ignore my presence in the room. I informed him calmly about my decision to go to India. He never looked up from his papers to make eye contact and answered just as calmly, "This may have consequences for you and there may not be a job when you come back".

This dart did not pierce my heart, I was well-prepared for his reaction and said with a firm voice, "I will take that risk; I have to take that risk. I'm very sorry for what seems to be an unprofessional decision, but it is for my own sanity and survival that I have to go".

"You may as well leave now", he said with a much stricter tone of voice, "My wife will take over your job for the time being, and then we will talk again after your return".

He continued reading the papers with his usual intensity and I left the room to pack up my things and return back home.

My train ride gave me time to reflect on what had just happened in the office and how easy my *temporary exit from work* came about. Was my boss prepared for my answer? Could he see that I was desperate to have time out from work? He knew me quite well and I had never let him down in the past. I felt a deep sense of gratitude towards him, as he made it so easy for me in the end to take time out. He must have asked his wife to help out in this crisis prior to knowing what my decision would be.

I was free to go to India. This was the right decision; I knew it in my heart and soul. My entire being felt light and happy, tingling with excitement; nothing and nobody could erase my smile.

All places that the eye of heaven visits
Are to a wise man ports and happy havens.

William Shakespeare, King Richard II

Stepping into the Unknown – Indian Diary

Knowing very well how quickly the mind distorts or forgets the truthful recollection of events, I decided to keep a daily diary of my experiences in India:

19th January 1991. Wake up at 5am fresh and in good spirits, the torment and challenges of the last couple of days put well behind me. All family members, my mother, son and our faithful dog, Max, see me off. I love them so much.

It is not the easiest of *Goodbyes*, as this is my longest, furthest and most unusual trip by far.

At 6am sharp, my dear friend, Gisela, arrives to pick me up and take me to the airport. What a blessing, it makes the beginning of my journey very easy. We collect two more ladies along the way, Laura and Rose. Despite the early hour, it turns out to be the jolliest trip ever to the airport. Both women have already been to see Sai Baba on several occasions and are able to tell plenty of anecdotal and even funny stories about this Holy Man, who seems to be endowed with a playful sense of humor. My curiosity about him is growing with every story I hear.

London Heathrow Airport. Security is unusually tight, I guess because of the looming Gulf War. In this chaos of suitcases and people, it takes us over two hours to check in, all under the protection of armed police and army personnel. I've never seen armed police at an English airport before. This must mean that our safety is under threat. Feel a little scared, to be honest. I have brief doubts about my decision to travel, but then recall all my reasons for going in the first place and feel secure in the knowledge that everything is as it should be.

Overcome with sentimental childhood emotions, I buy a teddy for company and comfort, but lose it before check in. How weird, where did that impulse to buy a teddy come from? Aged 41 now, my childhood days are long past. It's time to grow up and lose the fear of doing so, I tell myself.

We huddle together, a group of fifty pilgrims plus our group guides and their helpers, and pray for a safe journey. Don't know what the other passengers think of this. I look around to see their reaction and feel a little embarrassed to pray in a public space. I am not accustomed to displaying my beliefs in an airport, surrounded by hundreds of people.

The indirect flight to Madras will take us via New Delhi and Bombay. I'm sitting next to an Indian couple in an Air India jumbo jet. The husband tries to communicate with me making gestures and asking, perhaps in Hindi, to help with some in-flight paperwork. Neither of them can speak English nor read nor write. Their passports reveal to my astonishment that she was born in 1952 and her husband in 1910. Shock, she is younger than me but looks like mid sixty, with greying hair, pale, lifeless skin and a sad, subdued expression on her face. He, in contrast, looks very strong and vital for his age. I conclude that his life must have been much easier than hers.

13:32pm. The enticing scent of a curry lunch is in the air and is severely disturbing my concentration. Just sighted the first poppadum. I love vegetarian curry, it suits my metabolism, lights a little fire for digestion in my tummy, makes me feel happy, pleases my taste-buds and I'm going to the perfect place to give in to my cravings.

I notice that another group member, a woman from Cork, is not a vegetarian. Tut, tut, why am I on my high horse just because

I'm not eating meat at present, actually for over fifteen years? Perhaps she needs it? Stop being so judgmental, Louise. I became an involuntary vegetarian when I was only two months pregnant. The sight and thought of meat made me sick. Although I grew up believing that I needed meat for a healthy life and a strong body, there was no way I could eat the stuff during pregnancy or afterwards. I have no idea why this happened to me, but I do not like to catch myself being critical about other people's needs and habits.

Blood red sunset at 14.20 pm. Of course, we are flying east and into the dark night. I am standing at the back of the plane looking out into the fiery darkness, while doing some leg, arm and back stretches. A small queue is beginning to form, to get a glimpse of the spectacular night sky. I feel the need to give my lovely space at the window to someone else and return to my seat.

Another Indian woman, sitting to my left, pours out her heart to me and describes the various aches and pains in her body. Advise her to do Yoga and yogic breathing techniques, something she has never thought about or considered doing. I find it quite puzzling that many of the Indians I have met in London have absolutely no interest in, or knowledge of, their ancient, health-giving traditions. I know mostly Westerners who have incorporated Yoga into their lifestyle. Perhaps we look to the East for our salvation and they look West.

The lights dim and it is movie time. I have heard a lot about the Bollywood movie industry, but I had never before the opportunity to watch a Bollywood movie. This is the story: Beautiful girl is out walking alone on a rainy dark evening (would she really be allowed to do this in India, I ask myself?) Five handsome, but bad guys move towards the girl and try to molest her. On comes a motorbike beauty queen in leather, equally as stunning as the girl she rescues, who beats all these muscly guys to pulp with Karate kicks and super-human strength.

I must have fallen asleep and wake up just in time for the next film: Young man loves stunning model. In 99.9% of the movie he tries to convince the rather naïve girl that he is the one for her. One moment they are dancing ecstatically in the mountains (they look like the Austrian Alps), next moment, they are running along a beach. Bad guy, posing as good guy, tries to interfere and steal the girl. He nearly gets her, but exposes his bad character just in time. The girl sees the light and recognizes her true love, whose determination and honesty finally wins. Phew!

I noticed the absence of kissing, cuddling and physical contact between the lovebirds, as this is a common and accepted feature in our Western movies. It all looks so innocent and respectful, just like in the days when men used to feel dizzy at the sight of a woman's ankle.

For the last three hours my head has been throbbing. I never get headaches. Long distance flying doesn't seem to agree with me. Perhaps I'm dehydrated. I go and get some water. Is it safe to drink? Well, I'm not in India yet.

Love the design on the interior airplane walls. The small windows are surrounded with a temple-like pattern. Printed all over the walls there are blue and white images of Lord Krishna and his followers riding on chariots through the clouds. I love it all and imagine what my living room would look like with that kind of wallpaper. I love everything Indian, feel at home, perhaps a past life memory.

Have a long conversation with the woman from Cork. She lives with her three children, but is separated from her husband who walked out on his family; divorce is at present not possible in Ireland. She tells me about the pain and difficulties of being a separated Irish Catholic woman. One day she was crying out to God asking for help, when she had a vision of Sai Baba who held out his helping hand to her from the sky. She knew instantly that she had to go to India and see him in the flesh. I am impressed and deeply touched by her story. In fact, it still amazes me that every single person in our group has a personal calling to see this guru, including me.

1½ hour stop in New Delhi. We are not allowed off the plane. Sitting restless and anxious in my seat, perspiring profusely as the heat is building up inside our plane, or is it the effect of the curry? It's still pitch black outside, which is a pity. I would have liked to catch at least a glimpse of New Delhi from the air.

20th January. 4.30 am. We continue our flight to Bombay. On arrival, we are hit by hot, humid air and a foul smell after entering the airport.

Toilet situation not so good. The very young Indian woman attending to *cleanliness* has her three little children sleeping under the airport toilet washbasins. How is she coping with life? I thought that I had problems. My heart aches at the sight. I leave a few rupees behind and feel sad in the knowledge that there is nothing else I can do right now. At least she has a job and her children are in a safe place for the night, I console myself.

I don't like the idea of being confined to the airport in a city I have heard so much about; perhaps I will come back to Bombay another time? We are heading in a smaller plane for Madras, leaving the millions of little Bombay lights behind us. I imagine the life beneath our feet, recalling interesting, vibrant images I had seen in documentaries about India.

We fly over a stunning mountain range into a deep red sunrise.

9 am. Madras Airport. It takes a long time to get going, as custom officers scan our paperwork with critical eyes and query our reasons for visiting India. Someone in the queue remarked, *"They are more bureaucratic than the British"*. Embarrassed laughter.

Quite a few group members have chosen to travel to Bangalore in taxis - Ambassador cars, very nice, highly polished and rust-free - but I want a bus ride. Lovely breeze. I sit by an open window; actually, there are no windows in our bus, just iron bars.

Enjoying my first impressions of India.

The rice paddies are luminous green. (Have to stop writing now, the road is too bumpy).

21st January. Arrival in Bangalore.
I am catching up with writing my diary.

India is approximately eight and a half hours ahead of English time, so it seems as if we have *lost* a day.

The journey from Madras to Bangalore is a feast for my eyes – drive past places from another time, a different century. Notice a tiny, pretty village, fires burning; strong unfamiliar smell fills the air. All huts built in a semi-circle around a very large grain mill made of stone, very picturesque. Women sweeping passionately the sandy ground, whipping up masses of red dust. Everything and everywhere looks biblical to me. Small homes covered with palm leaves. Entire families, several generations perhaps, peering out of their one-room accommodation greeting the day, simplest ways of living, looking very appealing to an outsider. Adults and children with lots of brilliantly white teeth, big smiles, staring at our passing bus, loud chatter, car horns, unusual smells, incense, fires, hand-painted billboards, amazing fruit and vegetables on display on wooden trolleys, cooking at the roadside, little stalls surrounded by chai (Indian sweet, spicy tea) drinking men, dead animals, dogs and cows, obviously knocked down by speeding cars or lorries, live animals, dogs, cows and goats wandering aimlessly across the road, gigantic banyan trees, palm trees, bizarre mountains, gigantic rocks scattered in the landscape, as if giants had played a stacking game with them, creating most precarious rock sculptures. Oh India! Your beauty is extraordinary!

Bumpy ride until 9 pm.

Our hotel in a green and relatively quiet part of Bangalore is a welcome sight.

Exhausted, hot and dirty from fine red dust, feelings of extreme happiness. Had a refreshing shower (notice camphor balls in gully to keep creepy crawlies, especially cockroaches from making a home in our room), followed by more curry. I'm sharing my hotel room with Laura and Rose. I think of them as sisters.

Never shared a hotel room with strangers in my entire life, but nothing and nobody can stop me from sleeping, not even the sound of air conditioning which I normally hate.

22nd January. Outing with rickshaw in Bangalore. I love this city with its trees, green spaces and old, slightly faded villas reminding us of the days of the British Raj. We stop in Mahatma Gandhi Road to go shopping. Our feet have hardly stepped out of the rickshaw when a group of disabled beggar boys, about eight to ten years old, approach us and ask for money. I feel totally inadequate and flustered in dealing with them. One of the boys is crawling on all fours, as all of his limbs look broken and twisted. He is touching my feet to attract my attention. My initial impulse is the need to let off a little scream, but I can just about control myself. What to do? We were told by Sandra and Aime not to give money, as many children are forced to beg for greedy, unscrupulous adults. Apparently, there are begging syndicates, misusing children in the most appalling manner. Buying food is the favored way to help, as it may ensure that the children will at least get something to eat. We buy a bag full of food and drinks from a small shop nearby and give it to the boys. I can see that they are under pressure to ask foreigners for money only. They look quite unhappy and disappointed about us handing out food supplies.

Just as well that I waited for so long to come to India. Don't think that I would have been able to cope or handle a situation like this in my younger years. Actually, don't know if I am doing so well right now. I am confused and pained and walk away from the situation, take refuge with Laura and Rose in a sari shop. The need arises to buy a couple of pretty cotton Punjabi suits to be able to change my outfit more often in this heat, in other words, *justified retail therapy*. Being fairly tall with broad shoulders limits my choice dramatically, as most South Indian ladies are quite delicate and smaller in stature. I guess with the steady stream of devotees and spiritual tourists coming to see Sai Baba, most shops also cater for larger Westerners and I find some less glamorous, but pretty outfits. A brief glance at saris left me completely ecstatic; the choice of fabrics and beautiful designs, the glitter, beads, patterns, golden threads woven into clothes…and the striking, fabulous colors are just magnificent.

Encounter Between Two Worlds

Have I been deprived of color all my life to have such a strong reaction to India?

Rose, Laura and me in Bangalore, India

I observe that I speak, think and write in superlatives, but this is exactly how I feel. Obviously, on the one hand, there are all these challenges imposed on me to do with poverty; on the other hand, there is this immense beauty that constantly bowls me over.

Back to saris. I don't have the courage to wear a sari at this early stage of my trip, just in case the entire construction would fall apart while walking along. I admire the graciousness of Indian women, looking like Goddesses in a piece of clothing, about five or six meters long, draped around their bodies, pleated in parts and thrown over their shoulders with elegance. Pure magic.

We enjoy another rickshaw ride. Get a huge buzz from zooming about the busy streets of Bangalore, a very green and pleasant city. Cows meandering on main roads and pavements, eating any old rubbish they can find, including plastic bags. Can't help being concerned about their digestive system. What a sight. I imagine London traffic in a similar fashion, unthinkable.

Back at the hotel we assemble for a group prayer and supper. Great excitement, as we are split into two groups of 25 people each, the *Blues* and the *Greens*. I'm in the *Green* group with a pretty and talented singer called Helen as our group leader. Aime is handing out a blue or green scarf to each one of us, with the instruction to wear it without fail at every meeting, and a ring with the image of Sai Baba, to pull scarf ends through.

Can't get to sleep at all.

23rd January. At 3.15am, I discover that Laura is not sleeping either. We start talking. She is telling me about her reasons for coming to India and her sincere wish to ask Sai Baba for help and guidance. I admire and envy her for this firm belief in her guru, and that he will sort out her life. Will I ever reach that point of trust?

Laura falls asleep and my mind wanders off to a topic, which had been puzzling me for some time, namely the odd conflict between spirituality and sexuality. I wonder how many spiritual and religious seekers suffer from it? Why is it so difficult for so many people to integrate the two, even in a loving relationship or marriage? Is it possible for spirituality and sexuality to run alongside each other in perfect harmony? Come to no conclusion, but hope that I will in the near future.

Fall asleep and have my first ever Sai Baba dream: he is standing in front of me, smiling and emanating love. Notice that I have a little door where my heart is, just like a mouse door in a cartoon. Sai Baba makes himself tiny and enters my heart through that door. He then grows inside of me and expands until he fills my entire body. I think, *You will never get out of here,* and wake up with an incredible feeling of bliss and a big smile on my face.

What makes this dream even more special to me is the fact that Sai Baba himself tells his devotees that we can only dream of him if he wishes it. I consider the dream to be an unexpected welcome gift.

5.30am. Delicious Indian breakfast, followed by a taxi-ride in a convoy from Bangalore to Puttaparthi in the State of Andhra Pradesh, about 170 km away.

Our driver is a very noble looking Muslim who has colored his hair and beard bright red with henna. It gives him a very dignified appearance. His command of the English language is excellent, as he has been chauffeuring English-speaking devotees for over 20 years.

I notice a group of women laborers at the roadside, sitting in bright sunshine next to a huge pile of rocks designated for road building. Even hard work like this is done in a sari, giving an air of grace to an otherwise very tough and manly job. All women look very thin and worn out, I guess from smashing rocks all day long in the glowing heat.

"A government worker earns 30 rupees a day", our driver tells us, "that is the equivalent of about 1 Dollar. A woman sitting beside the road, breaking stones into small pieces for road building earns 2 rupees a day".

Shocking! Can they feed themselves or their families with 2 rupees? There is no end to the emotional rollercoaster. I feel like a girl in puberty, one moment my mood is up and the next I am devastated. How can I have equanimity when life presents itself with such gigantic differences between the rich and the poor, between the suffering and those who appear to have an easier time of life?

I am sharing the taxi with a couple from Kinsale, Ireland, she is Irish, he is English. We can't talk. Car engine is loud, no air conditioning; boiling hot inside our Ambassador car and outside; red dust fills the air and settles on my white Punjabi suit. I feel hot, sticky and dusty, but all smiles and happy! The road we drive on is often reduced to a single lane dirt track. Our driver treats the oncoming traffic like a bull, as though it was the red clothes of a matador, going for full-on collision and then, last second, moving speedily to one side or carrying on regardless, letting the opponent do the move. This calls for nerves of steel, or closing one's eyes frequently and hoping for the best.

Driving past women working in fields looking like exotic flowers in their bright, colorful saris, white bulls with painted horns pulling carts, elephants and bulls being washed in water reservoirs, lots of laughter and splashing. Have butterflies in my tummy, as if I was in love. I am in love, with the world, with India and everything around me.

Arrival at one of the symbolic entrance gates to Puttaparthi. We get out of our taxis to pose for a group photo. The gate is magnificent, two angels holding the Sarva Dharma emblem, symbolizing all major world religions. One could perceive it as glorious kitsch in soft cream cake tints, but I love it. All around us fields and the occasional cluster of tiny houses, people and animals.

On entering Puttaparthi High Street, I notice large signs on both sides of the road with sayings from Sai Baba, like, *Help ever – Hurt never* or *Love All – Serve All*; short and memorable phrases, often quoted by devotees.

Encounter Between Two Worlds

HELP EVER - HURT NEVER street sign, Puttaparthi

We carry on past Sai Baba's first University and Primary School buildings and a rather utopian building, shaped like an atom. The unusual architecture impresses me. I didn't expect these kinds of buildings in a small village which is almost unknown by the rest of the world.

Driving through yet another magnificent gate, the scenery changes and we now see small wooden trolleys and stalls with coconuts, fruit and vegetables, women sitting on the ground with beautiful flower garlands for sale, shops with books and pictures of Sai Baba, large crowds of foreigners, men mostly dressed in white, ladies daringly colorful, meandering through the busy main street, chatting, obviously out on a shopping expedition.

Finally, we have reached our destination and my heart jumps as we drive through the ashram gates. I catch a glimpse of the Mandir, or temple, where Sai Baba resides; it resembles an architectural creation out of *1001 Nights*. Surely, I'm in heaven. Everything I see has this *Wow effect* on me, I can't believe my eyes. Despite thousands of people milling around, there is a wonderful feeling of peace and serenity.

It is hot and dry in Puttaparthi. After a long, tiring wait outside the administration office to be allocated a room, I am sent off to the fourth floor in one of the *round houses*, circular buildings with inner balcony walkways all around each floor. There is a central garden, open to the sky, filled with interesting plants and flowers, especially bougainvillea, cascading down over several floors in vivid pink and purple.

Shock, our room compares to a prison cell, but without the comfort. It is completely empty, not even a chair or cupboard. Previous occupants must have left the room in a hurry and I'm glad that I had brought lots of cleaning material. My only consolation at present is the beauty outside. It doesn't matter; I am not here for worldly treats. Ashram equals monastery and a monastic life is modest, it has to be.

Share the room with Laura, Rose, Helen and Nancy. Having a massive cleanup as a team is first on our agenda. Out comes the bottle of disinfectant to scrub the floor and toilet/shower room, little creatures everywhere, fast and nasty looking. Not quite like home. I will survive, I'm determined!

We need to go shopping too for bare essentials. Stepping through the ashram gates into the main road, we are hit by noise and the mad hustle and bustle of rickshaws, cars, animals, shoppers and sellers. To my surprise, most shopkeepers are Muslims from Kashmir, not Hindus. They set up their businesses, selling anything, from beautifully embroidered fabrics and clothes to precious jewelry, small trinkets and statues of any size of Buddha and Hindu Gods like Krishna, Shiva, Ganesha.... We walk quickly through the village, avoiding all temptations and focusing on our immediate needs only.

We buy mattresses (filled with horsehair, so I am told) for 100 rupees (about 3 Dollars) each, and various other necessities, like pretty Indian bed sheets, pillows and bottled water. Many Indian helpers with endearing, friendly smiles are at hand to help. In fact, they have been patiently waiting for us to end our shopping spree. For a few rupees, all our stuff is being carried to our room, a service most welcome in this midday heat.

Encounter Between Two Worlds

Glad to be inside the ashram again and to leave the world with its business behind, a contrast I have never felt so sharply. Entering the ashram is like walking into an oasis of peace. Not surprisingly, this place is known as the *Abode of Supreme Peace, Prashanti Nilayam*. You leave the world outside and heart and mind calm down in an instant.

The Mandir (temple) looks like a giant birthday cake made from pink, blue and cream-colored icing, with the early evening sky reflecting the same delicate scheme, as above, so below. I am speechless and mesmerized by the beauty and tranquility around me.

Our first *Darshan* (seeing the guru and getting his blessing) with Sai Baba is close. We hold a group meeting near the Mandir and pray for an interview with him. We are reminded that this is why we are here, to have a private audience with a Holy Man.

Laura and I volunteer to help Linda. People in wheelchairs and with disabilities have an allocated section in this vast compound. We are lucky to get a place in the front row, Laura on the left and me on the right-hand side of Linda's wheelchair, facing the Mandir sideways. We take our place on the ground and wait patiently amongst thousands of women.

Devotees outside the Mandir in the Ashram

Darshan with Sai Baba

Women and men are strictly kept apart during Darshan, to avoid any distraction from the spiritual path. Men are seated at quite a distance away from us, on the other side of the Mandir building. Have to strain my eyes to see them. Perhaps I shouldn't be doing that anyway?

Hope I get a chance to hand over all the letters I was given back in London to Sai Baba. People write to him and ask for help with regard to any aspect of their life, including finding the right husband, wife, house, car, wanting healing for oneself or a loved one, the list is endless.

This is my first encounter with a Holy Man and if I am honest with myself, I do hope that he acknowledges my presence in his ashram. Sai Baba walks in a straight line towards our large group of sick and disabled women and briefly looks at the three of us, while continuing to move on. What a stern, severe look from big, dark, beautiful eyes. I feel no bigger than Thumbelina. How is it possible that this slight, delicate being appears to be like a giant, with an aura that fills the entire compound and beyond? Time stands still while he *floats* past us, all waiting for personal recognition, a smile, a look, invitation to an interview, blessing for a newborn, to give him a letter filled with hopes and wishes or to touch his feet. He moves through the crowds, throwing sweets, manifesting Vibhuti (sacred ash), emanating mysteriously from the palm of his right hand and taking letters, but not mine.

I feel like an abandoned child. Am I not worthy of his attention? OK, there was the look in our direction, should I be content with that? Was I hoping to be treated differently, just because I am helping someone else? How can I be sure of giving a selfless service? Am I making my life difficult, as usual? Well, I'm here to find out, to learn all about everything, but especially myself. This is a healing place, a spiritual washing machine and I am tempted to compare myself to a piece of dirty, stained clothing.

Meeting with Sandra and Aime, at 7.30 pm. Although we have only just arrived, our group desperately wants an interview with Sai Baba, just like everyone else in the ashram. What can we do to please him, to attract his attention? More prayer, more selfless service, more…? I feel dead tired, rejected and have lost my appetite. Sit alone under sparkling stars, opposite a tall statue with a giant lotus on top, a symbol of the flowering of consciousness. It is peaceful here, beautiful. I tell Sai Baba all about my fears and worries, hoping that he can hear my mind across the compound. I always maintained that I would never follow a guru, a living being, as if dead masters are wiser than living ones, but I feel that he pulls me like an invisible magnet.

Lights out at 9pm. Sleep from 9pm till 3.45am.

24th January. We quickly get up and go to Morning Prayers, or Omkar. I haven't felt so fresh and awake for a long time. It's a lovely morning. Only a few birds are chirping in the trees. I sit quietly in one of the straight, long rows of waiting women, a short distance away from the Mandir.

All around us is the sound of rustling saris and the patter of feet. No chatter. The atmosphere is electrifying, charged with expectancy. It is still dark, I have lost contact with the others and I am somewhere at the end of the women's queue. Not sure what happened next and why, but suddenly, we all get up and rush towards the temple. We sit down again, silently waiting outside the inner sanctum. Then, another rush, this time the doors to the temple are open and we move inside. My heart jumps with joy. As I walk inside, I see to my right, at the back of the temple, a large, life-size statue of Lord Krishna the Charioteer, spurring on his horses.

Louise in front of a mural of Krishna and Arjuna

Turning to face the front, I can see life-size statues of Sai Baba and Shirdi Baba, who, so I am told, was Sai Baba in a previous life.

I am giddy with happiness and feel that I have entered heaven, but that I have also brought my human torment with me to be inspected by the Gods. I shall ask the heavens if I can leave it all here, in a safe place, locked up for eternity.

The chanting of twenty-one OMs, the cosmic, primordial sound, starts the Morning Prayer, followed by Shanti, Shanti, Shanti – Peace, Peace, Peace. I have read that each OM has a healing effect on our inner organs and that the silent space in between the OMs is as important as the OM itself, as nothingness contains everything. I take a deep breath to fill my entire being with the sound of OM.

The strange, haunting voice of an elderly Indian woman continues with a song, or prayer, about Easwaramma, Sai Baba's mother, and, I guess a prayer for all mothers. I have goose bumps. Eyes closed, my soul is immersed in the vibrations of the song.

More prayers, then everyone leaves the temple to line up for a walk through the ashram, while singing devotional songs. I watch the procession from a distance. Have to digest the morning experience and be still. To speak in a metaphor the *inner bucket is overflowing*.

I can hardly keep up with events. There is so much time, but no time. All new impressions have to be assimilated. Feeling fulfilled and happy, empty and sad, low and high, lonely and part of nothing and everything.

At Darshan, Sai Baba was very quick in choosing a group of Indians for an interview. He sadly didn't choose us, but we have high hopes that our group will soon be asked to go for an interview. To be truthful, I am beginning to feel a little stressed about this urgent need for an interview. I feel like an undeserving child, trying to get attention and a reward for a good deed I haven't done yet.

I learn from London devotees that Hindus believe in Ganesha, the Elephant God. Apparently, he is the remover of all obstacles between God and man. He is childlike and innocent and can persuade the Gods to help us, if all else fails. Although I have some apprehension about praying to him and asking for a favor, I decide to follow the example of many Indians and circle the very large statue of Ganesha eighteen times. While many people are walking and praying, others, I believe mostly Hindus, are cracking coconuts in half, a gesture symbolizing the letting go and surrendering of the ego. I am praying intensely, whilst walking mindfully around the statue, asking for Ganesha's help to get the much-desired interview.

Louise with statue of Ganesha

Have the urge to smile and congratulate myself for adapting with ease to a previously alien culture. On my solitary stroll around the ashram for orientation purposes, I notice a number of blackboards placed strategically where devotees would pass. Entitled *Thought for the Day*, the same message is written on all boards throughout the ashram and renewed on a daily basis. These meaningful excerpts are extracted from Sai Baba's lectures and translated from Telegu, the local language, into English. Devotees love these *Thoughts…* as they often appear to be relevant to their own personal journey.

Today's lesson is strangely appropriate to my own thought process.

24 January 1991 – Thought for the Day

Service brings out all that is great in Man.
You are born to serve, not to dominate. It is only
when Man is filled with the spirit of service, that
his divine nature is revealed. He then experiences
the peace that passes understanding.
Baba

How can I be of service?

I don't know what time of day it is, Muslim prayers have just started. The wonderful sound of the muezzin, calling the Faithful to prayer, is coming from the mosque in the village of Puttaparthi. I enjoy being surrounded by a multi-faith community. In fact, there are people from all faiths right here in the ashram, Catholics, Protestants, Jews, Buddhists, Muslims, Hindus, Jains, Parsees, agnostics, even atheists and others…

We are all here together in peace and harmony. Can I call it a miracle? We are also here to find answers to our questions in moments of contemplation and inner peace, but sometimes that peace is interrupted.

New arrivals of devotees from the UK bring news of the Gulf War. For me, it is a reminder about my work and how glad I am to be far away from it all. For our Jewish organizers, Sandra and Aime, there is the constant worry about Saddam Hussein's threat to attack Israel. I don't dare to ask about their friends and relatives, but I can imagine the terrible uncertainty and fear for their loved ones.

Another group meeting in which we exchange our experiences of the day ends solemnly, as we have not had the longed-for interview. In fact, this may have become impossible. We are informed that Sai Baba has left the ashram without warning and without telling his devotees where he is going. People say that this is typical. He never publicizes his whereabouts and we are left behind to find him, once again.

I feel deserted – why am I here? Will I see him again? Sandra and Aime tell us that from now on we have to be spiritually even more disciplined, doing more service, helping out in the ashram canteen and kitchen, for example. This results in me feverishly chopping buckets full of onions, carrots and cucumbers, and washing up more plates than I have ever seen in my entire life. Surely, this will secure my place in heaven or at least in Sai Baba's interview room?

I remember that he says to all of his devotees "I am always with you". Does he mean that he is in my heart, or mind, always? Does he mean that I do not have to be with his physical form?

"I am always with you". Yes, that sounds nice and feels comforting, but what is the real meaning? I have come a long way to be with the physical presence, to experience what a guru is all about, everything else is too abstract for me at the moment and I do want to ask him so many questions about me, my life, my purpose.

The ashram energy has gone from buzzing to being totally subdued. Many devotees have left, because our guru is no longer in Puttaparthi. Have they followed him? Sandra and Aime suggest that this is our chance to work on ourselves and prepare for his return. At first I was grateful for this opportunity and for the space to look deep inside myself, but after taking a second glance at this situation, I have to admit that I am getting restless, upset and ever so grumpy, possibly undoing all of my Karmic credit.

I decide to sit alone in contemplation for a while, but my silence is interrupted by thousands of birds returning from their day trip into the countryside, making a mighty racket and taking refuge for the night in the giant trees inside the ashram. Strange phenomenon, there are plenty of trees outside. Do they know that this is a special place, a safe haven to recharge our worn out batteries? A half moon decorates the clear, star-filled sky. I look up and fix my gaze on the largest sparkle, searching and hoping for answers.

25th January. Getting up at 3.45am for Omkar, Morning Prayers, starting at 5am. Now Sai Baba has gone away, all longing to sit in the front row has left me and everyone else too. Our ambitions have burst like a bubble. No more push and shove in the Darshan lines. I sit in the second row this morning, my legs and feet very uncomfortable. Cannot find peace anywhere, least of all inside myself.

Difficult group discussions take place about being valued, our inner struggles and on losing trust that we are really looked after by a higher or divine force.

Our American roommate Nancy made a thought-provoking comment. She said that we are all just like beggars, because we always beg God for something: a new wife or husband, a new car, passing a test or winning the lottery, and so it goes on. This is so true. We go from one desire to the next, as if God is the biggest department store in the universe.

I am so restless and unhappy. Get together with a handful of other people and decide to leave Puttaparthi and go in search of our guru. We meet with strong opposition from other group members. However, in the end, we manage to get everyone's blessings to leave, but only if we promise that one of us will come back and inform the others of Sai Baba's whereabouts. Of course we can give such a promise easily, if this is our ticket to wherever he is. I am relieved and delighted. I didn't travel nearly 5000 miles to relax in an empty ashram as if it was a holiday camp, without a Holy Man, without my purpose for being here in the first place.

26th January. Five of us, Helen, Laura, Rose, Jamie (the only male, aged 18, a good looking young man with very long hair, a member of a rock band) and myself, rent a bus with driver and travel to Sai Baba's ashram at Whitefield, near Bangalore, hoping that he might be there. This is a big adventure for me. Thank God my mother doesn't know about this little detour. Our bus is literally held together by faith, but that is sufficient to help us reach our destination.

Judging by the milling of thousands of people in the streets of

Whitefield, we conclude that Sai Baba must be here. We take all of our belongings from the bus and go straight inside the ashram. People are lining up for Darshan and we join them after dropping off our bags. Our timing could not have been better. We must have done the right thing. Our joy is boundless.

We discover that today is a Bank Holiday and a special program has been planned. Instead of the usual Darshan, we squeeze into a long lecture hall and sit very close to Sai Baba's chair. He arrives, filling every atom of space with his presence, walking around slowly, looking lovingly and with a big smile at the crowd. Two young boys give a speech about his greatness. Then an older Indian gentleman also gives a rousing speech, but I am not able to take it all in, my mind is racing, possibly trying to match my heartbeat. After the talk, I listen, without any comprehension, to Sai Baba's long lecture in Telugu, translated by one of his University teachers into English. I just focus on his face; his big, deep, dark eyes in particular, the softness in his voice, his strange and mystifying hand gestures.

One story catches my attention, it is obviously important for me to remember. Sai Baba says, "If a man doesn't work, he can't claim a good pension, but if a man works and pays his contributions, he will get a good pension. That's the same with the universe. If we don't work on ourselves, have no discipline, we don't get the reward we want".

I'm working on myself. Wish I could shed all unnecessary, unwanted and un-serving layers of my character at once.

We find a room in Whitefield village for the night, in an Indian shopkeeper's home. The kind couple must have given up their own bedroom to accommodate us. Laura and Rose share a double bed and I sleep on a 1960s style, extremely narrow, curved, red PVC-covered couch. I am exhausted from the day and go straight to sleep, lying on my bed like a tin soldier. Keep waking up many times. Think I hear the sound of beautiful chanting and drumming all through the night. My mind conjures up a wonderful image of Hindu priests sitting around a fire and beating their drums. I have the urge to join them, but never make it, never find the energy to get up, as I fall back into deep sleep.

In the morning, I ask my hostess about the priests and the wonderful drumming and chanting I've heard in the night. She looks at me totally puzzled and possibly a little worried about my sanity.

"Sorry Madam, no priests, no chanting". She takes me by the hand and leads me outside, pointing out something I had completely overlooked when we checked into our *Hotel*. Literally just behind the house stands a huge factory. A big drive shaft or gigantic sledgehammer is crashing down repetitively night and day, but miraculously, my mind had turned all industrial sounds into a beautiful chant. Was this one of Sai Baba's miracles, just for me, perhaps a sign of his hospitality and a *Thank you* for my efforts to see him? Who knows? One thing I am sure about is this, I could not have slept a wink if I had known it was only a mechanical noise that kept waking me up – it would have driven me crazy.

After the morning Darshan we manage to get a room inside the ashram and call ourselves lucky, as large numbers of foreign and Indian devotees try to find a place to stay. The ashram quickly fills up and in my opinion reaches bursting point.

27th January. Lining up for Darshan. Tens of thousands of people are here today.

I have still no intention of worshiping a living being, and yet, something stirs my heart and soul when I catch the first glimpse of his orange robe. He literally floats through the masses of people, chatting, smiling, emanating love, throwing sweets, taking letters and manifesting Holy Ash for some lucky people.

Sai Baba hands out items of clothing to a large number of Indian devotees, then he starts feeding the poor. Hundreds line up to be fed, many of them children, the poorest of the poor. Everybody gets a big banana leaf as a plate and vast amounts of rice and dal (lentils), apparently an extremely nutritious food combination.

I observe children playing with the drinking water tap in the ashram compound, laughing and splashing, as if the tap was a novelty toy. An elderly Indian man notices my curiosity and explains that many villages do not have running water, that's why the children make the most of their time in the ashram. (Sai Baba instigated a gigantic drinking water project in 1994, as the Indian Government had refused to take action, connecting over 700 villages to clean drinking water in the drought-stricken State of Andhra Pradesh).

Monkeys are jumping from rooftops, screaming, playing games, stealing people's food out of their hands and dropping down from trees on to a plastic roof with a mighty bang. Total pandemonium. This entire racket stops in a split second when Sai Baba appears. Nature goes into silent Meditation. How bizarre?

After Darshan, Jamie is chosen as our messenger, returning to Puttaparthi by taxi with the good news that we have found our guru in Whitefield and to pick up the other group members. I very much look forward to seeing them all again in a day or two!

4.30 pm. Strong, sweet smell of incense surrounding us. I'm observing a mother with her disabled daughter. Seen them both before in the ashram in Puttaparthi. Always admired the apparent expression of love between them.

Sai Baba appears in the compound. To me, he conjures up the image of a rising sun, or a cool breeze on a boiling hot day. He walks slowly past us and the thought pops into my mind, *Please let me see beyond your human form.* At that very moment he turns around and looks at me for the very first time since my arrival in Whitefield. My inner barriers break down and I cry from the depths of my heart. Rose offers me her shoulder to cry on. What am I crying about? I don't even know, but a heavy weight has been lifted off my heart. Weltschmerz? (Melancholy or world-weariness) No, I'm bursting with happiness, but I'm crying and realizing, that the way I feel right now is exactly like the sentiments expressed in all the books I have read and felt ever so critical about. Has my heart been opened today to a greater, more universal love?

Encounter Between Two Worlds

A little Indian girl is sitting next to me, drawing Baba's feet on a notepad with the help of her younger brother. She realizes that I am crying and quickly sketches a present for me, the OM sign.

OM sign

The symbolism of this gesture means a lot to me, as I had just at that moment been thinking about the beginning line of Genesis in the Bible:

In the Beginning was the Word…

Darshan is followed by more speeches in the lecture hall. Have a turbulent experience. A German woman, sitting right behind me, starts swearing, cursing, accusing and complaining about Sai Baba. She is very angry.

I find myself getting upset about her anger, asking her to consider the possibility that she may be responsible for her troubles and only has herself to blame for her misery. No response. Perhaps she has taken drugs? She looks troubled and out of control.

People say that most gurus, spiritual teachers and Holy Men attract seriously troubled souls who often display this kind of behavior in the safety of an ashram and in the presence of their chosen teacher. When she/he responds disapprovingly for one reason or another, the devotee reacts with anger and blames the guru for all kinds of horrid things. In extreme cases these outbursts can seriously tarnish the guru's name, even when they are completely innocent.

Sai Baba frequently tells his devotees that he reflects our own self-image back at us. What we see and experience is only a reflection of ourselves; and when we point a finger at others, three fingers are pointing back at us. Scary stuff, when I think about all the office gossip I take part in. I conclude that nobody should be excluded or cast away from a holy place. Jesus didn't cast away Judas. He showed nothing but love and compassion. The angry German woman has every right to be in the ashram. All I need to do is to stop myself from getting roped into her angry world, from reacting to her dilemma.

28th January. I eat so little here. Feel like a fish in water, my body is light and buzzing with energy. Why do I need so much more food back at home? Is it the stress, the weather, the city environment that makes me desire calorific food?

Did some Yoga to counterbalance the many hours of sitting in Darshan. Sometimes I wonder if my legs will be bent forever after this trip. Not used to sitting cross-legged for such a long time, 3 to 5 hours in one stretch. Have slight ache in hip joints and knees, but my back is holding up nicely. Perhaps the years of Yoga practice are paying off?

9am. In a random fashion I open a book I bought in the ashram bookshop, *Teachings of Sai Baba*, to see if I receive a special message for today. The title on page 75 is *Divine Love and Surrender to God*.

Once again, the topic is totally appropriate to my current mental ponderings, about yet another subject that has puzzled me for years. On the one hand, we are supposedly the creators of our own universe, on the other hand, we are asked to let go and let God do the doing. Where does our ability to act end and when does God take over? Is it all in God's hands? Or is it all up to us? Do we have a choice? Or is everything pre-destined?

The sentence in the book that struck me most is as follows:

Surrender to God means to leave everything to His will and this is the highest form of Divine Love!

Surely, this cannot mean that I should sit in my armchair and wait for direction? What does it mean? How can I surrender my will? I have to make big and small decisions on a daily basis. They seem my own decisions, or are they? Please, can I have an answer?

Sitting with Laura and Rose in Whitefield. The British originally settled here due to a more favorable, milder climate and gave Whitefield its name. We just had a sweet coffee and dosas, pancakes filled with spicy potatoes. I am still not tired of Indian food; on the contrary, I love it more and more.

We are all dressed in white, with strongly scented jasmine flowers in our hair. I feel feminine and graceful, happy and healthy. Have loving thoughts about my little family, my son and mother, wishing they were here with me to share the experience.

The sudden flapping of wings very close to my left ear gets me out of my dream state. A mynah bird has landed on a bicycle in front of me. We look at each other admiringly for a while. *You know who you are*, I tell the bird, *and I envy you for that.*

Sai Baba gives us only a very brief glance today. He waves and goes. He often has a very busy daily schedule, meeting up with Indian and foreign politicians, Heads of State, Royalty, religious leaders, doctors, teachers, pupils from his schools and University, but also poor people to give them food and clothing. And then, there are the thousands, sometimes tens of thousands of devotees who come from all over the world and who also want his attention, preferably, an interview. He tells us that *Inner view* is more important, but I am human and long passionately for this elusive *Interview*. Have to be honest with myself, no good denying my desire to talk to him, be close to him.

I have this empty feeling again. Observing myself in all of the lows and highs, I conclude that this is probably an essential part of us, of me. I recognize a pattern. Well, to paraphrase Isaac

Newton, *What goes up must come down*. How right he was, as this law of Physics also applies to our inner experiences. What a rollercoaster ride of emotions we go through on a daily basis.

Let me enjoy the process, I tell myself, *let me play all parts well, the highs and the lows.*

The rest of our group finally arrives from Puttaparthi. It's great to be united again. Perhaps we will now be granted an audience?

29th January 1991 - Thought for the Day

**It is the Atma (Soul), that sees through the eyes,
hears through the ears, handles through the fingers,
moves through the feet. That is the basic you.
That You, is not elated by praise
or defeated by blame.
Baba**

29th January. I'm sitting in bed reciting a healing prayer when surprisingly negative thoughts flood my mind about the safety and wellbeing of my son and mother. I ask Sai Baba for guidance and hope to find some inner calm.

I also remember the words of a New Age teacher called Paul Solomon: *To worry means to waste your time with something that might never happen.*

Why then, do I spend so much time worrying? In my sleep I am once again gripped by what I fear most. I guess transformation on a deep level takes a bit longer than just one bright, sparkly moment in time.

Anxiety dream: I am standing in a street near home, in Croydon, observing my son doing his driving test. He is trying to get into a car park, driving up a dangerously steep slope. The street and slope are icy. Boris's brakes aren't working and he shoots down the hill. I am screaming, *Boris, Boris*. He crashes and I know he is dead.

Wake up shouting, *Boris, Boris* at 1.15am. Sweating profusely, heart pounding, crying. Start to breathe deeply in Yogic fashion, controlling the breath to a certain rhythm. Feeling peaceful after a while and go back to sleep.

My son is about to have his first driving test on the day of my dream, and the roads in England are snowy and icy; this I know from other British devotees. I have not been able to call home for a couple of days. Making calls from India is still rather difficult, there are only a few call centers and often all the lines to England are busy. Will have to go to Darshan in a minute with my heart full of worries about my son. Could there be a deeper meaning in all this? Do I have to learn, now, this moment, *to let go and let God...?*

30th January. 8.15am. Lining up for Darshan in the bright morning sun. To my amazement, I feel very composed and deeply still. This is incomprehensible to me, after such a turbulent night.

Our group is for once silent, none of our usual chitchat while waiting for Sai Baba. A female Sevadal (Seva=Service, dal=voluntary helper) stops in front of our long line of women, shaking a small bag filled with number tokens and Helen, our group leader, pulls out a number two. Helen is directed where to sit and we follow. We are all in the front row. I sit next to Donna, a lovely girl in her twenties. She has a brain tumor and her doctors have given her a maximum of six months to live. She starts drawing OM signs in the sand; it inspires me to do the same. Have this inner wish that our OM signs will attract the guru's attention. I guess I still think that I have some control over my destiny.

The sun is blazing, burning our faces. My sari is keeping me warm like a thermal quilt. I can feel little streams of perspiration running down my back and legs.

Our eyes are fixed towards the big gates in front of Sai Baba's spaceship-like home. The orange robe appears. I perceive a subtle movement around me, backs straightening, hands in prayer and then we fall into total silence. He comes out of his compound and walks straight towards us, then stops in front of Helen, asking where we come from and how many people are in our group.

Hearts are pounding; I can hear them, expectations high.

"We come from the UK, Baba, twenty five in our group".

Then the miracle happens! Sai Baba says with a gentle, soft voice "OK, come for interview. Go."

We can hardly grasp what has just happened. The Sevadal motions us to get up and go. I rush to collect Linda in her wheelchair, trying hard to walk with composure as I am wearing a new sari.

The Sevadal hurries us on, "Quick, quick, before Baba goes back".

I push the wheelchair as fast as I can through the gate, feeling awkward in my sari and hoping that the big safety pins are in the right places.

What joy and bliss. This is happening to me, to us, our group. We gather on a garden pathway outside Baba's Mandir. The garden is magical, with lots of little creatures, hamsters, rabbits and birds. Beautiful rose bushes and other flowers bursting into full bloom.

Sai Baba arrives and motions to me to push Linda in her wheelchair up a long ramp leading into the house, past him. I feel dizzy. Drama unfolds; the wheelchair will not move over the doorstep. My inexperience shows up, the wheelchair is rolling backwards as I am not strong enough to push it forward. I feel like dying on the spot.

Linda's husband, who stands with all the other men, comes to the rescue. He has to roll Linda's wheelchair all the way back and let everyone else pass. We spill into a big hallway, spot a large circular room and make a beeline for it, only to be told by Sai Baba that it was the wrong room. He smiles and redirects us into a tiny room. It is a very tight squeeze. I feel incredibly lucky, as I take my place on the right hand side of his chair. Can't get any closer.

Our interview group is a mixture of Indians, an Italian couple, Colombians, Ugandans, Yugoslavs and our multi-national group from the UK, in total possibly over forty or fifty people. I'm usually in the habit of counting anything, even the members of an orchestra, but numbers do not matter so much to me today. We all have happy smiles on our faces. We have reached our goal; we finally have our long-awaited interview.

(Seventeen, yes, seventeen years after this interview, just as I started to write this chapter of the book, I was given an *illegal* tape recording of our interview with Baba. As nobody was ever given permission to take a recording gadget into an interview, a group member had smuggled a small recorder inside his shirt pocket and captured the entire interview. Afterwards he gave a precious copy to my now husband, (we married in 2009). I had no idea that such a tape existed. My husband was in my group in 1991 with his late wife. We had totally lost contact after our trip to India and went our separate ways until a few years ago when we unexpectedly met again, after his wife had passed away. When I told him that I am in the process of copying down the interview part from my diary and have difficulties filling in the gaps, he emerged from his office with the tape recording. I am very close to calling this a *miracle*, as I know of no one in our group, or any other group, who has such a tape. Some passages of the recording are too personal to be published and are meant for the individual only, as Sai Baba clearly gives us an indication that he knows about our private lives, in detail).

Sai Baba sits down and asks, "Where is God?"
Most people have a quick answer, "In the heart, Swami".
"No", he replies, "The heart is only small. God is everywhere. He is omnipresent. He is everything. What is the way to God? Love, is the way to God". He answers the question himself and smiles.

I am drinking in the sound of his voice. Have I ever heard a sweeter, gentler voice?

Swami asks Aime: "What is your religion?"
Aime replies: "I'm Jewish, Swami."

Swami: "There are no *Jewish*, all are one, all are one. There are no differences."

(I believe that such remarks are not made to rob a person of their identity or to insult them, but to make them aware that self-identification can be the cause of conflict. Swami promotes harmony and oneness of all beings).

Aime asks Swami a personal and spiritual question. On a previous visit Swami had materialized a ring for him with the image of Christ. Protestations from Aime made no difference to Swami who told him that he would change the image when the lesson was learned. However, Aime's Rabbi was not too pleased or impressed, as he kept wearing his ring with devotion, trusting in the relevance and importance of what the ring symbolizes.

Today must be the day of Aime's transformation, mission accomplished. Swami takes his ring, blows on it, yes, blows on it and changes the image from Christ to something else. I cannot see what the image is, perhaps the Star of David.

Another devotee asks: "Some people today believe in the Fall of Man, that we are human beings now, but that we come from Angels".

Swami: "Not Angels".

Devotee: "…and that we have a Devil; and we have a God".

Swami: "Everything is God. Where is God? God is everywhere. Everything is God. You are also God. With you – in you – around you. Physically, you are a man. You are not that. You are **That**, which is Atma".

Devotee: "Yes, I understand, but how can we tell people that there is no such thing as Fallen *Man*?"

Swami: "Wait for the conscious state to arise in them. Don't worry…it's just a play".

Baba focuses his attention on an Italian woman. Turning to a very large pile of letters he has collected from devotees earlier during Darshan, hundreds of letters in fact, he picks out the very letter she wrote to him, from about the middle of the pile.

'Aaaah', everyone in the room is impressed. Swami, without opening the letter, speaks about its contents and why it was written.

"You have cancer", he tells her, "Swami will help".

He pushes the right sleeve of his orange robe up to his elbow, perhaps to show us that this isn't trickery, starts circling his right hand, palm facing down. I first see a light appear in the center of his palm, and then an object emerges…a see-through plastic bag containing long red pills.

Aaaah, even louder than before.

He catches the bag with his left hand and tries to open it, but can't. He jokes: "Swami can make the bag, but he can't open it".

Laughter.

He hands the bag to her husband, a gentleman in his early sixties perhaps.

"Take twice a day", Swami instructs her.

Then he circles his right hand again and this time, we can see the manifestation of a very large lady's wristwatch. The dial is at least four centimeters in diameter, with a gold surround and three long, black cords with big golden beads as straps. It fits perfectly. The woman is beaming with happiness and gratitude.

Swami tells her: "When you are back in Italy you will forget what Swami has told you and that I will help you. The watch will remind you every day. Westerners like looking at a watch".

Laughter. Then Swami turns once again to her husband: "Don't be jealous, because I give her so much attention, she needs help, she will be OK".

The husband smiles and nods knowingly.

There are several Indian Ministers present. Swami takes them into an even smaller private interview room. He leaves the door wide open, perhaps for me to witness even more miracles. As I am sitting right next to the door, I am privy to another act of Love.

First he diagnoses one of the ministers, telling him that he had cancer of a certain type (I cannot understand what type). The man agrees with Swami's diagnosis. Then, the right hand circles, again a glow of bright light appears in the center of Sai Baba's hand and a Shiva lingam, an egg-like shape that Hindus use in their daily rituals and worship, manifests. Swami instructs the minister to pour water over the lingam during his daily prayers and drink the water several times a day, to help his cancer. I can feel the love Sai Baba is showering over this very sick man, the love of a most caring mother. This Love is a tangible presence, seemingly boundless, unconditional, sweet and beyond our understanding of human love. I feel very privileged to be in this prime position, from which I can see and hear everything.

At one point Baba looks smilingly at me and says: "Big Eyes, look away". He must know perfectly well that I am totally mesmerized and cannot, will not, take my eyes off him. The fact that he calls me *Big Eyes* thrills me to bits, as I had heard that it was a gift to be called a special name.

Throughout the interview Sai Baba repeatedly says that he holds everything in his right hand. (This reminds me of one of my favorite songs 'He's got the whole world in his hands...').

Swami manifests rings for the college boys who are also present and who express their devotion and reverence in a most heart-warming way.

And here I am, witnessing one miraculous manifestation after the other, as if they are a completely natural occurrence. I do not have the slightest doubt that everything I see, hear and experience is done out of pure Love, with a capital L.

I am standing right next to one of the Indian boys and Sai Baba. He has both of his very tight sleeves pushed up to his elbows when he creates yet another ring with his image. I could have easily been a doubting Thomas, but somehow, Sai Baba did not need any of these miracles to convince me that he is indeed a very special being; he does what he does regardless of what anyone thinks. I feel very blessed to be a witness. All manifestations aside, the biggest miracle is the immense, tangible, never ending stream of Love flowing from him to one and all.

A devotee asks a question, "The Atma never dies and is never born, what is it that goes on to the next life?"

Swami: "That is Consciousness...there is no life, there

is no death; from conscious comes conscience, then comes consciousness. Everything is coming from consciousness…(gap in recording). This is my body, but what is real? My senses? But you are not the body, not your senses…"

Swami continues: "Everybody is God; in you, within you, around you. That is God. Physically, mentally there are many differences. But inside, all is God…the best way to know God is to Love! Love, Love, Love".

After my initial struggle with his physical form, and it is only a form – a shape he has taken, I feel more at ease and look beyond the form. I now know now what he stands for…Love. Love All.

Our group is invited to squeeze into the tiny personal interview room. Not everybody fits inside. Again I sit right next to Swami.

I am so happy to be so close and to be able to witness everything that happens from close-up.

Swami focuses his attention on our youngest group member, Jamie, and his mother. The young man wants a blessing for his rock group back in London, but has it pointed out to him that he is not keeping good company. Jamie looks disappointed, as Sai Baba is relentless in telling him that he has to change his ways and not cause so much grief to his mother. Sex, drugs and Rock 'n' Roll are leading him in the wrong direction. The mother smiles gratefully at Swami. Many more personal things are said, all of them meaningful to me, as a mother. It is as if Swami is talking to me, but I, for some reason cannot open my mouth to ask any questions myself. I just look and listen.

Swami tells us that it is an auspicious full-moon day today, a very special day.

My initiation day, I think to myself!

A woman from Ireland is told that he knows that her husband has another woman and that she has lots of worries, but not to worry, Sai Baba will help her through the crisis.

He keeps pointing out that many people in our group have a lot of secrets and that he will see us all individually at another time.

Sai Baba made us laugh by pointing out that: "Self is good, fish is good, but selfish is no good".

With the wave of his right hand, he manifests Holy Ash, or Vibhuti, and distributes it amongst us. I eat some of it straightaway, believing in its healing properties and place another portion in a paper tissue, to be taken home to my mother and son. I want them to benefit from this interview and the manifestation of this special Vibhuti.

Swami indicates that our time with him is over. He fetches a red shopping basket filled with Vibhuti bags and hands them out to each one of us, beaming with joy and love, like a Mother handing out sweets to her children. Before we leave, Swami promises to see all of us again.

(I have been told that this does not necessarily mean he will see us physically in another interview. It could mean that he would appear in a dream or any way he chooses, in any time span he chooses).

I still have this burning question I want to ask, about last night's nightmare in which my son crashed his car, but I am not able to open my mouth to form a question. I stare at Swami, stand still for a moment and look into his eyes. He says: "Go now", taking me gently by the arm and directing me towards the door. It is time to leave this sacred space and Sai Baba's physical closeness.

End of interview.

My heart sinks, as I did not find the courage to ask my most important question. Part of me feels blessed and happy, and yet, another part of me is in agony because of the dream about my son.

Let go and let God. Please, Louise, get a grip! I create my own unhappiness out of fear and I am telling myself that it is possible to undo this fear, simply because I can recognize it. While walking slowly back to my dormitory, I notice that my mind is running on parallel tracks. One track is leading to a crisis and the other possibly to freedom. Surely it should be easy to choose the right one, but is it?

Sai Baba says that it is easier to manifest trinkets and gifts for devotees from the palm of his hand (and we may call these manifestations *miracles*) than to transform the heart and mind of one human being. But when this transformation finally takes place, **a real miracle is happening**.

I can see the truth in this statement. **We are the miracle! I am the miracle!** The manifestation of trinkets is of no consequence or importance, they are just a gesture of love, but our transformation of character is what really matters!

A rickshaw ride to Bangalore with my new friends, Laura and Rose, gives me hope of finding a working telephone. I try for an agonizing hour to call the UK, but it is impossible to get through. With every failed attempt my inner voice is shouting out at me to stop worrying, to surrender to the situation. Deep in my heart I know that I am *looked after* and so is my family. This is Sai Baba's promise to his devotees when they come to see him. Trust Louise, trust.

We decide to relax in a smart hotel with a cup of spicy masala tea and talk about our interview. How believable is this? Three middle-aged ladies from England sitting in India, sharing in a matter of fact way our memories about miracles and impressions of a most unusual morning, in fact, the most incredible, unbelievable morning of our lives. I'd love to tell my family all about it, now, but we have to take the rickshaw back to the ashram without being able to make that call.

Our *Green* group is meeting up on the rooftop of one of the hotels. Each one of us is asked by Sandra and Aime to give a personal account of our interview. There is one common denominator in all of our stories; we all felt the infinite, unconditional outpouring of love. Our guru is just that in my eyes, pure Love. Love on two feet!

Radiant, auspicious full moon, illuminating the night sky. Time to retreat, as lights are switched off at 9pm. Earlier in the day we had to move to a different room. Now we are 8 people sharing a small dormitory, tightly squeezed together. There is the Indian mother I so admire with her 13-year-old disabled daughter

Indi, a middle-aged American called Sharon and five people from our group, Laura, Rose, Nancy, Helen and myself.

The room is hot and stuffy. Indi, the disabled girl, is very restless and her mother frequently bursts into loud prayer to calm her daughter. I recognize my inability or better, my inner block, to deal with disabled people in a natural, uncomplicated way. My apparent shortcoming is upsetting me and I send a heartfelt prayer to heaven, asking for help.

Restless night, my awake state gives me plenty of time to reflect on the day and my life. In desperation I try to recite a newly learned Sanskrit prayer. Sai Baba recommends that we keep our mind occupied with spiritual matters, rather than giving in to what he calls the *monkey-mind*, which likes to create havoc and confusion. Focusing the mind either on prayer, through meditation or visualizations, apparently has the same effect as focusing on our breath. It leads to stillness and inner calm.

I love the sound and vibration of all the Sanskrit prayers I have learned so far, but it is the Gayatri Mantra in particular that pulls me like a magnet. This prayer has been handed down by the Gods thousands of years ago, I've been told, through the Rig Vedas (Hindu Scriptures) and, although I have no concept of its power and true meaning, I feel compelled to recite it until sleep gets hold of me:

Gayatri Mantra

OM BHUR BHUVA SVAHA
TAT SAVITUR VARENYAM
BHARGO DEVASYA DHEEMAHI
DHYO YO NAH PRACHODAYAT
OM SHANTI SHANTI SHANTI

Translation:
Supreme Lord, the source of existence, intelligence and bliss,
the creator of the universe.
May we prove worthy of thy choice and acceptance;

> May we meet thy glorious grace.
> We meditate on thy transcendental light.
> Please illuminate our intellect and lead us unto righteousness.

31st January. I must have prayed myself to sleep. Feel exhausted and not ready to get up, but push myself to conquer yet another day of unknown greatness and full of surprises.

6am. A large crowd of people living outside the ashram has already gathered in the courtyard. We assemble in the dark, form a not so orderly queue and walk, a few musicians leading the way, through that part of the village that is located behind the ashram walls and not seen from the main road. I would never have ventured here on my own; in fact, I had no idea that this community of many tiny huts, some more substantial than others, existed just a stone's throw away from our ashram life.

The absence of street lighting makes walking on an uneven dirt track quite difficult. Some clever people have brought their torches to light the way; they must have done this before. I observe that only male villagers are up and about, or, perhaps only men are visible at this hour, chatting and drinking chai served from tiny market stalls equipped with just a kettle and a glowing fire. I can smell the sweetness and spice and wish I could just go and get a cup for myself.

Our path is uneven and stony; it's hard to keep walking blindly, while clapping and singing at the same time. Find myself stumbling along with a big grin on my face, as I can't help singing the song, *If they could see me now…* inside my head.

All along the ashram wall, on the main road, there are wooden tables with goods for sale during the day. I notice that many of the stall keepers actually sleep by the roadside on the ground, underneath their market tables or some of them on top. Where are their homes? Do they have a home? Have they travelled from afar to sell goods to spiritual tourists? The mysteries of the Indian way of life are boundless.

Although I manage to control my feelings and anxiety about

my son quite well, there is still an occasional ripple of unpleasant adrenalin rushing from my tummy up to the top of my spine.

Surrender, surrender, Louise, that's the only way.

Finally, before going for breakfast, I manage to make that all-important phone call to my mother. All is well in the universe, no accident, no problem, no dramas occurring at home. Only one little hiccup, my son failed his driving test. Phew...I can live with that.

I return to the Ashram to sit quietly under the giant, ancient banyan tree, to reflect on my emotional state and to say a big *Thank You* to the heavens for everything. Tears release themselves. I sit and cry, grateful that my dream about my son's accident was only a dream and not a premonition.

Yesterday, the 30th January, appears as if an entire week has been squeezed into one day. In retrospect, there are quite a few extremely puzzling aspects of our meeting with Sai Baba. So much of yesterday's experience was totally out of the ordinary. The interview was crammed with moments that were pushing the boundaries of my thinking to previously unknown dimensions. What appeared to be several hours in his presence were in reality only thirty minutes of worldly time. How is this possible? And how come I understood so much of Sai Baba's interaction with other foreign or Indian devotees, which must have taken place in another language, possibly Hindi or Telegu? And what about all those manifestations I have seen: Shiva lingam, rings, pills, a watch, Vibhuti? Everything seemed matter of fact and totally natural, as ordinary as buttering a sandwich. My mind is spinning.

We had not seen the other half of our group, the *Blues*, for quite a while, as each group go their separate way. The disappointment is obvious to see in everyone's face. Why did only the *Greens* get chosen for an interview? Don't know. But then, we still have nine days left, plenty of time for everyone to be selected for an interview.

For some bizarre reason it feels like a very personal rejection when Sai Baba doesn't acknowledge our existence in an obvious, demonstrative way. It must be like a father/mother singling out one child in favor of another and the deep hurt is felt like a dagger piercing the heart. But when he finally does see us, acknowledges us, gives us love and attention, we are elated, happy, ecstatic, complete and in Seventh Heaven. What utter nonsense? How can we possibly achieve equanimity if we have these countless attachments, including to our guru, who is patiently trying to convince us that we should not have any attachments?

1st February. Very restless night. Sharon, the American in our dormitory, wakes up screaming. Torches switched on. We all look at her with sleepy eyes, bewildered about the racket and wondering what it is all about. A monkey has crept into what is supposed to be the Fort Knox of mosquito nets. Sharon had barricaded herself into the net to avoid such an encounter, but the curious monkey obviously loved the challenge and was determined to climb into her bed. The poor creature is just as frightened as we are and makes a speedy escape through our open window. It takes a while for the excitement to die down and even longer for me to get back to sleep. Our room is hot and airless.

1st February 1991- Thought for the Day

Service is Worship. Each act of service is a flower placed at the feet of the Lord and if the act is tainted with Ego, it is as if the flower is infected with slimy insects. Who will contaminate the feet of the Lord with such an offering? Have NO egoism while you serve the people.
Baba

Ouch, harsh words from our guru. Have to think about this *Thought for the Day a* bit more than usual.

I no longer believe that everyone comes here to be cured by Sai Baba. Some people just wish to find the grace to die in peace, and that has to be alright too. Isn't that a miracle, when we come to terms with our mortality without a fight, and when we are able to smile at death when he comes to pick us up? What a fantastic achievement.

Feel the need to write about a member of our group who imprinted herself deeply and dearly into my mind and heart. It is Donna, who was sitting next to me when we were picked for our interview with Sai Baba. She is 21 years young, has been diagnosed with a brain tumor and given only a few months to live. How is it possible that a young woman, so sweet in character, determined, strong, patient, dignified…can be so ill? Some people may say that this is her Karma, her body reacting to actions of the past, in this life or a previous life. She is setting an example for all of us, carrying on without grumbling, no complaints or bitterness, no *Why me?* She is smiley, composed, and yes, even happy.

Wonder what it feels like to have only a limited amount of time left on this beautiful planet. I notice that I have lots of attachments, loved ones, pets, places, collector's items…would I be ready to let go of life? Well, possibly not, but if I had to, this would be the perfect place to learn to surrender to the inevitable.

2nd February. Darshan. Sai Baba is throwing mountains of sweets, mostly to men. They respond like children, even those with silver hair, scrambling excitedly for lost sweets on the ground. I enjoy watching the scene, giggling to myself. Nancy from Singapore, who is sitting next to me, has a logical explanation for this. She thinks that the reason for his gesture is because **men need to be sweetened.** I'm sure she speaks from experience and I nod in agreement. It must be a special day for men, as only men, Indian men to be precise, are called for an interview.

Eunice, one of our group members from Ireland, kindly offers me a bed in her hotel room for one night, just to have a good night's sleep and to get away from our noisy ashram dormitory. I gratefully accept the offer and it works out fine, until...

3rd February. Sleep beautifully and deeply until 4am. Our group has agreed to have a day of silence. Leaving Eunice's hotel room to go to Morning Prayer at about 4.30am without saying a word to her. The village is already alive and buzzing with activity. The smell of fried Indian food, chai and incense fills the air, women sweeping the pathways. I breathe in deeply while taking careful steps in the semi-dark.

Being accustomed to chatting away at any hour of the day, I'm feeling strangely uncomfortable only two hours into the silence. Feel the need to talk to someone about not talking. Sitting in the Ashram compound, writing my diary and wondering why Eunice is nowhere in sight. It is getting very late. The music has started, indicating that Sai Baba is on his way. Then I catch a glimpse of her, running quickly to take her place in the Darshan lines, her face luminous red, looking at me furiously. Found out later that I had locked her in her hotel room by mistake and she had to shout for help, breaking her vow of silence. I am so sorry!

Today I have a secret, I even feel reluctant to write about it, but I will, as it is part of my soul journey. I am helping in the Western Ashram canteen, chopping mountains of vegetables for hundreds of lunches, washing dishes, and feeling grateful and happy.

Nobody knows where I am and I'm not going to tell anyone where I've been. Baba's *Thought for the Day* on 1st February about *Service* shook me in my comfort zone. I realized that often in the past I did things, good deeds, not only to help others, but also and possibly foremost to get praise and to please my ego. What a shock. How does one become a selfless person? I want the service I am doing today to be just for God, self- and ego-less. So be it!

3rd February 1991- Thought for the Day

**You have earned this human birth by
virtue of your past good deeds.
This body is given in order for you to serve others.
Therefore, we should undertake sacred works in order to
sanctify the body given to us.
Baba**

How appropriate the *Thought for the Day* is to my situation. Do the heavens know what I'm thinking? Doesn't it say quite clearly in The Bible *Ask, and you shall be given?* Perhaps The Bible is not suggesting that we pray to be given a new car, house or partner, win the lottery etc., but that we are given answers to our spiritual questions, our soul questions.

4th February 1991- Thought for the Day

**The supreme meaning of service is that you
have to realize yourself through yourself.
If one realizes who one really is, one becomes everything.
Baba**

4th February. Ooohhh...today's message feels like soothing honey trickling down a sore throat. *How close am I to knowing who I am?* I ask myself. The thought of becoming one with everything sounds most uplifting and comforting.

Meet a Californian, John, while queuing at the accommodation counter. He and his brother had an interview with Swami only two days ago. I tell him how happy I felt about their good fortune. Sai Baba had manifested a ring for John, not without first giving him a lecture on how to mend his ways and to tell him that *"...the heart is not a couch on which many people can sit"*. The ring is studded with diamonds in the shape of a cross. John explains to me that the center diamond fell out yesterday and that his heart chakra, or heart energy point, has been hurting ever since. Then, as luck would have it, he found the diamond again. John is very certain about the deep symbolic meaning of this occurrence. Affairs of the heart had always been a problem for him in the past. Now, with Swami's help, he feels confident in being able to tackle those difficulties.

Darshan. We are sitting under the gigantic, beautiful banyan tree in the middle of the ashram compound. Baba is upset with his devotees for stampeding during the line-up for Darshan. Everybody wants to be close to him and first in line. Devotees quite frequently forget their manners and go wild. Sai Baba loves discipline, but most Westerners seem to dislike it intensely. We think of it as an infringement on our freedom, but why? What would be achieved without discipline?

Here we are, undisciplined devotees, greedy and craving for his attention and breaking the rules of the ashram. Swami is upset with us and this might result in a short, sharp Darshan, his eyes penetratingly darting around like balls of fire. Is this his Shiva aspect in full expression? I love it and I smile to myself!

5th February. Still no further interview with him.

"Don't ask for Interview, ask for Inner-View". How many times have I heard these words? I notice that I call Sai Baba all manner of names, endearments, just like other devotees. My attitude to him has changed. I have accepted him as a teacher and feel comfortable with that, simply because I have learned so much just by being here, listening to him, watching him. The love and goodness expressed in everything I hear and see is evident. Only a good teacher can come up with a saying like the following:

There is only one Religion - the religion of Love,
there is only one caste - the caste of humanity.
There is only one language – the language of the heart.
There is only one God – He is omnipresent.
Let the different faiths exist, let them flourish and let the Glory of God be sung in all the languages and in a variety of tunes. That should be the ideal.
Respect the differences between the faiths and recognize

> them as valid, as long as they do not extinguish
> the Flame of Unity.

This is music to my ears, as I am also a firm believer in unity in diversity and the oneness of all things and beings.

6th February. Laura and I go for a long walk up the dusty, busy main road to eat in the Indian Ashram canteen, for some reason situated at least half a mile away from the ashram itself.

We stop at Krishna's makeshift cloth tent at the roadside. Krishna and his wife are seated on the ground; he is playing an Indian harmonium with the stumps of his hands, singing songs of praise to Lord Rama, Lord Krishna and Sai Baba. Krishna has lost all of his fingers and most of his feet to leprosy and yet he is smiling and singing his heart out.

Here is a human being whose body is eaten alive, has no belongings, nothing to call his own, except his devotion to God. How humbling. I hope that the memory of this encounter will always stay fresh in my mind.

We walk on and come across an injured puppy. His throat is slit, blood spilling out of the deep wound and I am almost sick at the sight, but not Laura. She grabs the little pup, sprinkling an entire bag of Vibhuti (Holy Ash, known to have healing properties) into the gaping wound. The dog runs off and the experience leaves me speechless. Head down and deep in thought we go to get some food. Actually, I've lost my appetite.

4pm. Sitting in the Lecture Hall for Darshan, thinking about the injured puppy and Laura's speedy action. She is so helpful and practical with all creatures in need and can jump to the rescue without a thought and do the right thing. I behave more like a paralyzed deer, unable to move or think about the next step. Why am I like this? What are my gifts? Do I have a secret ambition to be like Mother Teresa, but can't quite get my act together? Somehow, I don't think that becoming like her is my path. I have a son and commitments to a different lifestyle. Perhaps what I do, the way I am, is just as valid. We can't all play the same part, have the same roles and character traits…

In a clock there are many wheels of different sizes, all working together in harmony. This analogy gives me comfort. Whichever wheel size I am, enabling this world and the universe to spin in harmony, perhaps I am perfect for *my* world the way I am, and my role is to do what I'm able to do, not more, not less?

Indi, the young disabled girl in my dormitory, gives me a lovely big hug today, dispersing my fear that I'm totally useless in dealing with her disability. Another breakthrough that gladdens my heart!

Just get over this need to feel emotions all the time, I tell myself in a strict manner. Beverley, the psychic healer in our group, tells me the same thing. I'm always responding emotionally to people and situations and get completely overwhelmed and exhausted by the impact. My soppy identification with feelings has never served me. HELP!

At least I can see my behavior pattern more clearly now, and perhaps this is the first step to eventually jump off this crazy emotional rollercoaster way of being.

7th February 1991- Thought for the Day

To become completely detached, it is not necessary to grow matted hair, wear ochre robes and torture the body into skin and bone. It is enough to do all acts as dedicated to the Lord, without any desire. This is the Secret of Liberation.
Baba

7th February. Our last day at the ashram. The *Blues*, the other half of our group, finally get their long-awaited interview with Sai Baba. Justice at last!

It is time to say *Goodbye* and Indi, the disabled girl, is upset and crying when our time comes to leave. She gives all of us a sweet and a bangle to remember her by. I thank the heavens for the opportunity to meet Indi and to learn from her! Indeed, I feel blessed and grateful for all the insights and experiences I had in the last few weeks.

Five *mature* ladies manage to squeeze into a small Ambassador taxi bound for our Hotel in Bangalore. Our convoy of at least 10 taxis is whipping up clouds of fine dust while travelling to our next destination.

Although all five of us share one hotel room, it seems utter luxury after weeks of simplicity in the ashram. Strangely enough, I've not thought about or missed any luxuries either.

We prepare to celebrate our last evening together with another delicious vegetarian meal, followed by an hour of devotional singing. Helen asks me if I would practice with her and even lead a couple of songs. I convince myself that saying *No* is not an option.

One of the songs selected for me is, *Shalom my Friend, Shalom my Friend, Shalom, Shalom,* a Hebrew song.

I have goose bumps. Of all the songs in our evening program this one was chosen for me to be the lead singer. Coincidence or Sai-incidence, as I now call life's mysterious happenings? Every time I try to sing *Shalom…* during our rehearsal, I feel my throat tightening, my heart jumping, emotions welling up and tears trying to emerge. I tell myself that I am only the instrument. *Let go and let God*. Somehow, my programming is working and I survive our evening celebration without my usual display of emotions. In fact, I thoroughly enjoy the singing and especially the finale to our evening. From the depths of my soul I sing the words:

> Shalom my friends, Shalom my friends, Shalom, Shalom,
> 'til we meet again, 'til we meet again, Shalom, Shalom.
> Shalom Chaverim, Shalom Chaverim, Shalom, Shalom,
> lehitraot, lehitraot, Shalom, Shalom.

I call my family in the UK to say how happy I am to see them again soon. Find out that the South of England is covered with one foot of snow, a very unusual occurrence. When I inform our group about it, everyone thinks that I am just joking.

8th February. Our journey from Bangalore to Madras Airport started on the wrong foot at about 3pm. There is aggression in the air. Some of us are falling out with each other…I'm not sure what's going on. Amazing that after so many weeks of introspection and living in harmony, quite a few people have the need to fight with each other.

Hello real world, we are back! Perhaps that's just human nature and too much love and peace can make you angry? Sadness overcomes me.

I think the argument started, because not enough taxis had been booked to transport fifty people to the airport in Madras. This will mean a very tight squeeze indeed, but several people have opted to set off on their own, in anger.

Six of us, including the driver, scramble into our taxi. Immense heat is emerging from the car engine, no air-conditioning. Some people don't like to drive along with an open window because of the dust. I am boiling hot and nauseous.

First I was in Heaven, now I must be roasting in hell. That's Life!

We are driving into the night, the lights of Madras nowhere in sight, but all of us hoping that Madras Airport will be reached shortly. Then, our taxi makes a sudden stop. I exclaim: *We are lost!* Our driver briefly leaves the car and confirms our suspicions on return. We have lost sight of the other taxis and have driven in the wrong direction for quite some time, even though our driver kept continually asking country folk for directions to the Airport. Obviously, nobody knew the right direction, but didn't want to seem unhelpful. This is the Indian way; if you don't know the answer, make one up to at least appear to be helpful. On another occasion I would have found this characteristic quite endearing!

We also find out that our driver can't read and has never

driven in this part of India. Hallelujah! The heavens have a strange sense of humor.

I recall seeing a sign to Madras some miles back. We retrace our steps and finally head in the right direction, praying furiously and with more passion than I had ever known in my entire life.

The unknown is so scary in the dark.

We only have half an hour left before the flight check-in closes. A mad rush starts, but who cares, we make it on a wing and literally, on prayers. Apparently, the part of the group that had found the way to the airport and had arrived early, had also been praying for our safe arrival, but some of the men still manage to react strongly and with a fierce patriarchal outburst on our involuntary late arrival.

Helen expresses an interesting insight on men, after observing the male responses to our delay. She thinks that, *when men are stressed and under pressure, their ego is being challenged and the first thing they do is to withdraw their Love energy. All efforts go into combat and aggression.*

Hmmm, interesting! This would of course explain why Sai Baba spends so much time and gives so much Love to male devotees. I notice that I spell Love with a capital L, that's because I mean Love with a capital L, nothing to do with our limited human understanding of Love.

9th February. 4am, arrival in Bombay. We are exhausted. A young woman in our group faints because she is totally dehydrated. The airport doctor has to come and inject fluids. We have been told again and again to drink at least two liters of water a day, but for people who are not accustomed to drinking water, but have only tea and coffee which are diuretic, this can turn into a real problem, especially in India.

Flight to London is ninety minutes delayed. Nobody minds. Exhaustion has turned us all into silent, demure creatures. As long as we get home safely, the world is in order.

I enjoy my flight meal and the wonderfully obscure Bollywood movies. I am ready to go home, tell my story, and talk about the miracles I've seen. Will they believe me? We'll see. I feel a warm glow radiating from the inside out, a happiness and contentment which I had no experience of before going to see my guru.

Where was I for the last few weeks? Was this a dream? I have learned and understood so much about myself, others, about Love and the incredible, magical mystery tour called life. I will never be the same again. I have woken up and it feels absolutely wonderful.

Feel overjoyed to see my son and mother and Max, the dog at the airport. What a wonderful, cozy, loving feeling, to be met by family! This is very special!

End of diary!

15

Peace-Story-108

Some colleagues, especially my boss's wife, the film editor who filled in for me while I was in India, greeted my arrival at work with some hostility. Everyone was exhausted and, I guess, polluted with images and the sadness of the Gulf War. Who can blame them for feeling upset when I had deserted the office at such a difficult time?

More than ever I knew that I had made the right decision. I had missed the entire war coverage, the 16-18 hour working day, the stress and the horror. To my surprise and delight, there was no talk about me no longer having a job. I took my place in the office as if I'd returned from a *normal* holiday.

The first news story to be edited by me was called *Peace negotiations*, 108 seconds long. I took this as a confirmation that I've returned to work at the right moment in time, as the number 108 is in itself of a deeper meaning. In the Hindu tradition the Japamala (string of prayer beads) has 108 beads. There are the 108 names of God etc. I knew for sure, that the number 108 was an auspicious number and my heart rejoiced.

The night before returning to work I had a very vivid dream: I was walking with some of my colleagues through a beautiful landscape, trying to make them aware of the magnificence around them and arouse their enthusiasm to come with me and join me on my walk. Their frozen faces and hearts rejected my proposal and my colleagues tried in turn to make me realize that I was deluded. I walked away from them, but did not feel lonely or isolated. In fact, I felt quite self-contained and strong, knowing only too well that it was not possible to share my joy.

I suddenly remembered this dream at work, and it seemed to me like a warning not to speak about certain aspects of my journey. The magical details were reserved for my friend, Gisela, who, in the last four weeks had read several more books about the Indian Holy Man, Sai Baba. In fact, she was thinking about the possibility of going to India herself. She was prepared and ready to listen to my colorful, almost unbelievable stories.

I was floating on cloud nine for quite some time and the stress-filled environment I had to work in, did not touch or affect me.

Life is not
about waiting for the storm to pass,
it is about
learning to dance in the rain!

(Anon)

16

Epiphany

About three months after my return to London, the long awaited VHS cassette of Aime's first enthusiastic filming efforts, made during the group's visit to India, arrived at my home. I had the day off work and thankfully, nobody was around to disturb a three-hour viewing on a floor cushion in the living room, with a large cup of coffee. To be able to re-live and re-visit this life-changing trip to India was an unexpected joy. There were so many things captured in the video, which I hadn't seen before or hadn't been part of, as the splitting up of our groups resulted in us doing different things at different times.

I learned that the Irish couple from the *Blue* group missed the long awaited interview with Sai Baba on 7th February 1991. They thought it would be unlikely that there would be an interview on the very last day of our trip and stayed in their hotel in Bangalore. One should always be prepared for his last minute surprises.

(I heard later that the couple returned to see Sai Baba the following year, had an interview with him and he manifested a beautiful ring for the wife. Swami told her to hold on to the ring in difficult times. Sadly, she died of cancer fairly soon afterwards. I am certain that he knew about her fate and that the ring must have given her strength and support until her last breath).

Almost three hours into the video and still clinging to my coffee cup, I sit cross-legged on my cushion, spine straight, ready to listen to the devotional songs performed on our last evening in India. I smile at my efforts, as my insecure, soft voice was constantly trailing behind Helen's strong and beautiful singing voice, almost like an echo. With every note she was emanating pure devotion. The last song, lead by me, the traditional Hebrew Blessing, commences: *Shalom my friend, Shalom my friend, Shalom, Shalom.*

The camera is focused on my face, singing this very emotional song. I recall being filled with an immense sense of gratitude, as I, the only German in the group, was chosen to sing a Hebrew song.

I watched myself, singing my heart out, with fascination and pride. After a quite a long time of steady focus on my face, the eye of the camera slowly pans across my shoulder towards a beautiful, mesmerizing, very alive photograph of Sai Baba.

Fixing my eyes on his, I move even closer to the TV screen.

What happened next was beyond my control and not in any way anticipated. I had this overwhelming feeling of *Forgiveness* showered over me, like a warm wave, flooding me with a feeling of love, freedom, relief, joy, understanding, an opening............... euphoria, bliss.

I use words, but they all have limitations. People describe their moment of liberation, or enlightenment, as indescribable. Well, I'm also struggling to express myself and to communicate the power of my experience. (This is not an experience of *enlightenment,* but purely of FORGIVENESS. I like to make this point, as it could easily be misunderstood).

Sai Baba's eyes were now filling the inner screen behind my closed eyes, gazing at me from the inside, with Love. Then, a cathartic wave of crying shook my entire being for over an hour. I've never cried before, not like this. What happened?

After the last tear had been shed, this immense sense of relief, of lightness, spread through every atom of my being. **I, Louise, was forgiven.** Who forgave me? Did the heavens forgive me? Who was forgiving whom and what for, in my case? Was I forgiven for an atrocity, like the Holocaust, I was never personally involved in, but for which I always felt some responsibility?

The power of the experience scared me for a brief moment. Could it be just an illusion? ***No, no, no!*** I had experienced too many heartaches, painful, joyful and meaningful close encounters with my Jewish brothers and sisters, to make my entire experience just an imaginary story. This is real. Something had just happened. The heavens had moved, perhaps because I had moved into a more aware state of consciousness, to show me what **FORGIVENESS** feels like. To finally forgive myself was an incredible feeling; it was **HUGE**.

In the Jewish tradition *Forgiveness*, with a capital F, is a business of two components. There is the perpetrator and the one who forgives, but the perpetrator also has to forgive him or her-self. Otherwise, who are we to forgive? Is it primarily God's prerogative on the day of the Last Judgment, if there is such a day? Can we forgive each other, here, now, no matter what crime has been committed, and what would forgiving do for us? Perhaps the notion behind forgiveness is the conscious decision to live in peace, not only with the world, but especially with oneself.

After all, one of the world's most loved Christian prayers, ***Our Father…*** refers to this subject: ...***give us this day our daily bread and forgive us our trespasses, as we forgive those who trespass against us...***

God, in my eyes, is Love, and where there is Love, there is no place for anger, revenge and hatred. And this eternal, unlimited force of Love, which I call God, had forgiven something to somebody, to me, and the feeling of gratitude and relief was beyond description, my joy out of bounds. A massive space of light had been created, where previously only dark, heavy clouds resided.

Who could I call and inform about my good news?

I sit in silence for a very long time, processing, digesting and internalizing what had just happened. Not a word will be said to anybody about this. That is my decision. This is too big for me to shout out into the world. Would anyone understand? I had found peace at a personal level and it had changed me profoundly!

When the road ends
and the goal is gained,
the pilgrim finds that he has travelled
only from himself to himself,
that the way was long and lonesome.

Sai Baba

Encounter between Two Worlds
– From Myself to Myself

More than a year later and missing the companionship of like-minded spiritual travellers, I'd decided to join hundreds of Sai Baba devotees in Crewe, England, for a 3-day retreat. Arrival time was around 3pm on a Friday afternoon, very organized and disciplined check-in and lots of smiley, happy faces.

I shared my room with my Irish friend, Eunice, who was also in the *Green* group in India. In fact, she was the one I had locked into her hotel room on our day of silence. She was like the sister I never had and I looked forward to sharing the next three days in her company.

Every single moment of our time during this weekend had been organized to perfection. All speakers and performances were given a fixed time slot; every minute was accounted for, from the beginning prayers to the workshops and finally, the Aarthi, a closing prayer.

A variety of workshops were on offer during the day and the one about the *Collective Unconscious* was one of my favorite choices.

Here is what Wikipedia, the Internet encyclopedia has to say about it: ***Collective Unconscious*** is a term used in analytical psychology, first described by C. G. Jung. It is part of the unconscious mind, expressed in humanity and all life forms with nervous systems and describes how the structure of the psyche autonomously organizes experience. Jung distinguished the Collective Unconscious from the personal unconscious, in that the personal unconscious is a personal reservoir of experience unique to each individual, while the Collective Unconscious collects and organizes those personal experiences in a similar way with each member of a particular species'.

Our workshop about the *Collective Unconscious* turned out to be most interesting and informative. It soon became obvious that our tutor was an expert on the subject, as he had captured our attention. And to further deepen our understanding of what we had just heard, we were put into small groups of 5 or 6 people to have a lively debate, followed by the second part of our lecture. I listened intensely to every word the tutor said. But suddenly, I could not hear a word, as if my head was going under water and my ears were blocked, my head was spinning and I was feeling dizzy. My body temperature changed from hot to cold to hot, I wanted to lie down, be silent and listen to the voice within. A very clear, soft, but firm inner voice was telling me to speak at the retreat about my personal German/Jewish experiences.

Who was talking to me? What was happening? I had no sense of fear about my sanity at that moment, as part of me understood the seriousness and importance of such a proposal. Most people have no time or sympathy for those who hear *inner voices*, on the contrary, but what was I supposed to do, ignore it, just because it sounded a bit spooky? This was a clear request, but from whom?

COLLECTIVE UNCONSCIOUS – was this the answer to my personal conflict? Had I taken upon my shoulders and carried with me, through my entire life, the collective memory of the horror of the Holocaust? It felt as if an explosion had taken place inside my head. Could anybody see from the outside what was going on inside of me?

Someone kindly asked me if I was alright. I nodded. I couldn't cry, although I would have loved to. Then my head emptied itself and I sat with closed eyes in this beautiful, full emptiness. *I sat inside Love!*

The workshop ended and I rushed out of the lecture room to avoid any kind of contact or conversation. I didn't want to speak to anyone about my experience; I just wanted to be alone and hurried back to my dormitory. The voice in my head persisted.

Doubts troubled my mind. Finally, I started to bargain with the heavens and came up with the following idea: *Should my story be of value and interest to anyone else in this world, I need a strong, clear, definite sign that I should speak in public. If the organizer of this event is the first person to cross my path when I leave the room, I will take that as a sign, that I have to approach her and ask for permission to speak.*

About what exactly, I didn't know. And anyway, this event was perfectly organized, from A to Z, there was no space for my sudden impulse. Besides, I had never given a public speech in my life and the mere thought freaked me out. Fear had caught up with me.

I gathered up my long scarf, wrapped it around me like a protective cloak and made my way to the canteen. Only about 20 yards outside, in the courtyard, the organizer was the first person to cross my path. She walked right in front of me, together with another woman, chatting away, totally oblivious to me hovering nervously nearby. My heart jumped out of its bounds. Nonsense, I thought, I can't possibly give a talk in front of almost 450 people. What would I say? Am I crazy for even considering it? I let the opportunity slip away and walked, heart still pounding, into the canteen, feeling quite annoyed with myself and most cowardly.

The inner voice was relentlessly grinding me down, *Ask for permission to speak, Louise.* Like a doubting Thomas, I was only able to summon up my courage after the third attempt. By then, I was totally fed up with my fickle behavior.

Let go and let God, I thought. *Ultimately, it is not my choice. If anyone wanted me to give a talk, let him or her organize it. It was not in my hands, nor was I keen to do it. This retreat was planned in advance from beginning to end and I very much doubted that a speech from some unscheduled participant could easily be fitted in.*

Slowly I walked over to the organizer's table. She was a middle-aged Indian woman, her thick black hair tied in a bun, strong upright character and slightly school matronly manner. She looked at me, smiling kindly, as if to say, *I'm really a very nice person. Don't be scared.*

"I hear this inner voice which keeps asking me to get your permission to speak at this event", I said clumsily. Silence. She looked at me for a while, "Do you have anything interesting to say?"

I was not prepared for this question and repeated it slowly and quietly. "Do I have anything interesting to say? I don't know", I replied, "I just hear this voice, which is getting louder and is not giving up. I have to ask you, if I can speak at this conference". Silence. Her eyes fixed on mine.

"OK. You have 20 minutes, tonight", she informed me with a benevolent smile.

TONIGHT! 20 MINUTES.

That's a lot of words and this was short notice, my panic-stricken mind informed me. I hadn't prepared a speech. What am I going to say?

I had dinner with my Irish friend Eunice and told her all about the dramatic events of the afternoon, and that I was allocated a 20 minutes' slot for my talk in the evening. Her response was very supportive and just what you expect from a friend. There was no questioning, no doubt, only trust that the right words will flow out of my mouth, without even having to think about them. *Thank you!* That's what I needed to hear.

Slowly, silently and in deep contemplation we walked through the courtyard towards the big meeting hall, for the evening's proceedings.

As always at these Sai Baba events, we could expect nothing less than a wonderful treat. Prayers, music, singing, theatrical sketches with a spiritual-moral message, inspirational and very funny speeches were on the agenda, filling the hall with joy and happy laughter. This was the problem, my problem, the longer the entertainment carried on, the funnier it became.

I had my doubts that what I had to say would fit in with the program. A story filled with human drama, tears and sadness was just not appropriate, so I sat on my chair, anxiety welling up inside of me.

Oh Louise, what have you done? Life would have been so much simpler, if I hadn't stuck my nose out and offered to give a talk. But then, who wanted to talk? My inner voice told me to do it. Not that I think of this inner voice as a different part, no, but perhaps the voice is that part of me which is in deep slumber for most of the time and ignoring it would be like missing the chance of a lifetime. The evening passed and I was not called up to give a talk. I felt great relief and disappointed at the same time. It wasn't meant to be.

On my way out, the organizer came rushing towards me, apologizing for not squeezing me into the Saturday night's program, but...

"You're on tomorrow, after the lunch break. You're our last speaker."

She left in a hurry and I was gasping for breath. Of course, what I had to say would have spoilt the evening's fun and would have been totally inappropriate. The *heavenly organizers* knew that, no doubt. Well, I just had more time to drive myself crazy with excitement and fear. Sunday morning came and I had butterflies whizzing around in my tummy.

The second and last session of the day started again with songs and prayers. I loved this part, it lifted my soul.

Please, please, God, let me be strong and help me not to cry when I give my speech!

"And now we have an unscheduled talk by Louise Illig", said the organizer and President of the Sai Organization UK, sending a big smile my way and calling me up to the stage.

Wow, the world looked different from up here. It could have been quite a daunting experience, if it hadn't been for this sudden feeling of deep inner calm falling over me, like a protective cloak. I felt strong and clear. Looking into the audience made me realize how many loving eyes were looking back at me in anticipation of what was to come. I looked at the men seated on the left hand side of the hall and women on the right, just as it is in the ashram. Words left my mouth slowly and carefully at first. I spoke of my life's journey and the pain I felt as a German, this lifetime, the immense Karmic burden I carried because of the Holocaust and how this burden was a suffocating experience, which held me back from being a free spirit until the day of my epiphany, sitting at home, watching a video about my trip to India. My eyes fell on a very petite elderly Indian woman who sat in the first row in front of me, crossing her fingers, whispering in my direction, "Don't cry, I pray for you, don't cry!"

I spoke for forty minutes, yes, forty minutes. That's twice as long as the initially suggested time. Nobody stopped my flow or reminded me that I had taken up too much time. Actually, I'd forgotten about time. The story was finally being told, in public. I noticed handkerchiefs, tears being wiped, noses cleared. Usually, as the reader very well knows by now, I can't stop myself from bursting into tears and feeling emotional, but everything was different this time. Words kept pouring out of me like a steadily flowing river.

Done. I had shared the biggest story of my life with hundreds of people. I believe approximately 450. People rose to their feet and gave me a standing ovation. I was in a daze, dream-walking and feeling light on my feet. **Shalom**. From all corners of the room, people were saying *Shalom*, moving towards me to hold my hands and to utter some magical sounding words in Hebrew. The hall was flooded with tears and emotion. I felt emptied out, solemn, calm.

I took my place next to Eunice who clutched several hankies in her hand, her face and hug said everything. I had to close my eyes until the end of the program. The organizers gave *Thanks* to Sai Baba for this fantastic retreat and to all the helpers and participants. The time had come for the final Bhajans, devotional songs and the Aarthi, the glorious and magnificent prayer that always raises the roof and makes my heart fly.

Women made their exit first. Slowly we filter through the

narrow glass doors on the Ladies' side of the hall while the men had to wait their turn. I emphasize this point, because what happened to me next was obviously an encounter in another dimension and could not have happened in *real life*, as there were only women present on my side of the hall at this moment in time.

Just as we had entered the long corridor, I noticed to my right a young man of slim build, about my own height of 5'7", distinctly Jewish-looking, with curly dark hair and beautiful, but sad, big, dark eyes, their size exaggerated due to thick lenses in his dark-rimmed glasses, making him look extremely serious. He didn't smile. His lips suggested that he wanted to ask me a question. Our eyes met. I must have stopped in my tracks and stood still while we stared at each other. I had not seen him here before and today was our last day; in fact, this was the end of our retreat. He looked somewhat out of time. His grey trousers were tight and too short, so was his jacket. All his clothes were much too small for him. He was somehow squeezed into them. The white sleeves of his shirt were gaping out under his jacket sleeves for at least two inches. Only one button of his jacket was closed with difficulty, indicating that it was much too tight. He had outgrown his clothes, but looked proud, clean, his shoes highly polished. He was staring at me and I at him. No words were exchanged between us, just penetrating, searching, intense looks. I don't know for how long.

There was something strange about this encounter. I was aware that I could see his entire body, although he was standing right behind where the wooden partition separates the corridor from the hall. In fact, the partition wasn't there during our encounter. I could not see it. There was just the two of us. The realization shocked me. What was happening here?

I elbowed Eunice and pointed in the young man's direction.

"Have you seen this young man before?" I asked her.

Startled and bewildered she looked at me and exclaimed, "What young man?"

"Well, this one, the one who is looking at me".

As mentioned before, my friend has the habit of blushing intensely when she gets excited or embarrassed. Her face turned crimson red.

"Louise, there is no young man. I can't see any young man".

"But I can see him, like I can see you. He is standing there, looking at me".

"Then only you can see him for some reason". She shrugged her shoulders, puzzled, but accepting.

Time stood still for a moment or an eternity. I was absorbing the image of someone who supposedly only I could see. The strangest, inexplicable sensation came over me, a lightness of body, a floating sort of feeling. I felt as if I was in a dream and in the real world at the same time while the young man and I looked at each other. I did not want to let go of his image, wanted to ask him questions, but I couldn't speak.

The crowd was now pushing me forward and I had to keep walking, but inside my mind, his image remained strong and clear. I could identify him, if I saw him again. Who was he? Why could my friend not see him? What had just happened to me? I could think of countless questions, but no answers.

Nothing prepared me for what was to follow. Outside the building, people, mostly Jewish people, surrounded me, shaking my hands, hugging me, thanking me, speaking in Hebrew, smiling at me, silently greeting me. I had no idea that at least a third of those present were of Jewish descent. My head was throbbing. Then, I felt a hand on my shoulder. A woman I'd seen many times before at Sai Baba gatherings came close to give me a big hug.

"Can we sit under the tree for a while and talk?" she asked me. We sat down, she held my hands and told me her story.

"I am Jewish. You are the first German I've spoken to in my entire life. I swore never to have anything to do with Germans and always avoided contact. Many family friends had to flee from Nazi Germany and settled in South Africa. Our family was not directly affected by the Holocaust, but I heard all about the atrocities committed by the Nazis. Some of my family members knew people who had died in concentration camps. I hated the Germans all my life. I don't know why I'm breaking this rule today, but I felt compelled to talk to you."

She thanked me for my moving speech, wished me well and left, but I grew roots under the tree. Eyes closed, I surrendered to the sounds and scents of nature, too fragile and shaken to move.

So my speech fell on fruitful soil. It wasn't in vain. I was certain that I spoke for many Germans who possibly had similar experiences and who were also struggling with the inherited memories of a very dark time in history. How do we heal the past? Can we, as individuals, contribute to healing? Today, NOW, at this moment, I feel that, *Yes, we can contribute to healing the past.* We have to start with ourselves and do our best to speak and live the truth from within. Encountering the Holy Man, Sai Baba, certainly gave me the strength and fearlessness to look at myself with critical eyes, to observe the good and the not so pleasing aspects of my character, and to wholeheartedly embrace all challenges with an open mind.

Before getting ready to vacate my room, I walked around the college compound in search of the young man who had suddenly appeared in front of me, hoping to find his face again amongst the crowd, but he was nowhere to be found. I looked, just to be sure, but deep inside of me I knew that I would never find him amongst the living.

He was a Jewish Ghost!

18

Another Moment Outside Time and Conclusion

Just imagine the implications of such an encounter, the incredible opportunity for being a catalyst in the healing process. I love the spirit of generosity and connectedness of all beings, which is implied by the idea of reincarnation, as it opens the doors to a much more tolerant approach to life. We may then find it in us to act in a more compassionate and understanding manner towards other people, despite the multitude of cultural, religious and ethnic differences. Who is the person you are looking at? Who are we truly? Have we all met before, in another life? Have we been enemies or friends, lovers, relatives?

As if the heavens tried to prove their point to me, I was to have a further encounter, when I would cross the boundaries of time and witness myself in another incarnation through a near-death experience.

A few months after my talk in Crewe, I was invited to hold a weekend workshop on spiritual growth in Bray, near Dublin, staying with my friend Eunice, who happened to be a practicing Reiki Master. After two and a half days of intense, but very enjoyable work, she offered me a Reiki session for relaxation and as a gift for my hard work. I gladly accepted the offer and lay down on a floor mattress for my treatment, closing my eyes and placing my arms alongside my body. Eunice started the session kneeling behind my head on the floor. She informed me that in her style of Reiki there was no physical contact at all during the session, and that her hands were quite a distance away from my head. I was aware of her close presence, as I could hear the gentle flow of her breath.

Suddenly, an extremely disturbing, unfamiliar feeling overcame me. I tried to move, but couldn't, tried to hold on to something, but couldn't, I felt disconnected, dizzy, not quite myself. Part of me was floating away, while I knew perfectly well that my body was lying on the ground, unable to move. Then came the shocking realization that I was slowly dying, and there was nothing to hold on to. I felt very frightened. Then, a strong sensation of anger and frustration arose and I had the realization, that I was dead.

Shit, I thought, *Shit, I am dead. This is not what I have bargained for. I don't want to be dead. I have too much to do.*

I panicked, tried to bargain for my life, worrying about my loved ones, my son, and then, out of nowhere came my decision:

Let go and let God.

In a split-second, all fears and struggles subsided and a fantastic feeling of splendor and grandeur took their place. I saw myself lying in a coffin, or stone sarcophagus, arms crossed over my chest, skin painted gold or bronze (the parts I could see, arms, face and feet), dressed in a beautiful, deep burgundy-red robe made of a rich, heavy fabric. My heart sang, my mind in a state of ecstasy and bliss. I became aware that there was someone else in the room, a warden. I lay in this state of bliss for quite some time, then, a window like a skylight, but made of heavy stone slabs, just parted above me in the ceiling. I looked out into the universe; the dark, star-filled sky, sat up, and gently floated out into space until I reached my destination. I had no idea where my journey took me. I *landed*, and a voice, unfamiliar but familiar, instantly started talking to me. It spoke softly and warmly and full of LOVE.

The *voice* informed me that it was not my time to stay here and that I had to go back to Earth, because I had a lot more work to do. Next, I was permitted to ask all the questions to which I wanted answers, existential questions about life and death and the meaning of it all. But sadly, the answers are hidden somewhere in my subconscious, I have no conscious recollection of them. All I remember is that I was sent back *on my mission* and awoke, still lying with my arms alongside my body and my friend sitting by my side.

She looked pale and traumatized. "Never do that to me again. What happened to you?" she shouted at me almost angrily. "This was v e r y scary."

"You tell me", I replied, still feeling dazed and not quite ready to communicate about the experience.

My friend then told me her account of what had happened and to my surprise, she had seen exactly what I had seen, or experienced, but from a different perspective. She saw my dead body (I was a man), which frightened her. She saw my arms, face and feet painted gold, the dark red robe, the sarcophagus, the strange room we were in and in which she was present as my male warden. Suddenly, there came a point when she lost contact with me, could no longer see me and became quite anxious and fearful. Time passed and then I was back in the room again.

My friend was shaking and in a raw state of emotions, unlike me, who now felt calm and composed, but very light-headed. We decided to sit in meditation for half an hour and somehow get over the shock of what had happened.

How can I explain this experience to anyone, including myself? Have I been shown a way out of living in fear about death and dying? I've experienced for myself that by *letting go and letting God*, letting go of my panic and fear in my moment of death, something much greater, something more beautiful and eternal was able to manifest itself, and that manifestation I will call *my true self.*

And that *true self* was radiant with Love!

Twice in my life I had been caught between two worlds. The experiences were as real to me when they occurred, as any other I may have had in my daily, ordinary life. Although I have not found a 100% foolproof explanation for either my encounter with the Jewish Ghost, or about my totally unexpected near-death experience, I know that I was deeply touched in both cases, right down to my inner core. Was I granted an inside look into the workings of our universe? Did I have these extraordinary encounters to trust completely in the possibility that I have had many lives and that I may also have been a German-Jew in a past life? That gives birth to the question:

Was I sent back into my body to be able to write this book and to help others along their journey?

Since my talk in Crewe, I had told no one about my encounter with the *Jewish Ghost,* or shared my strange near death experience in Ireland, but the memory of it all remained a vivid and important part of me. Eventually, I plucked up the courage to tell my son and my husband (as mentioned previously, I had re-married in 2009). Both of them proved to be hugely supportive and encouraged me to write about these *out of the ordinary encounters*. I always had and still have a strong sense that what I have to say might have relevance and a place in the hearts and minds of other people, souls who struggled and still struggle in the same way as I did.

Who was the young man who appeared to me in Crewe? Never did I come across a photograph of him or find any other evidence for his existence. After reconstructing the event in my mind time and time again, I established that it was totally impossible for him to be present amongst the women, as the men had not been able to get even close to leave the hall at that point in time. I was one of the first of over two hundred women to go from the main hall into the long corridor. A further indication that something inexplicable had happened was the fact that when I saw the young man, I was able to see him *through* a several feet high wooden wall partition with glass units at the top, as if the entire structure didn't exist. My experience or vision had no physical boundaries, it happened outside space or time.

In desperation to find out if there was a foolproof explanation, I spoke to a psychic and author (*Tales of Two Worlds*) from Tunbridge Wells, England, a wonderful woman in her eighties who has since passed away, Peggy Mason. She had gained respect and an almost enigmatic reputation in the world of psychics and had written many books and articles on the subject of psychic phenomena.

I pinned my hopes high that she was the right person, perhaps the only person, to help me shed some light on this extraordinary experience. I wanted her to *tune in* to the image of the Jewish Ghost, in order to find out who this young man might have been, and summoned up every ounce of courage to contact Peggy and tell her about my encounter. Expecting her to jump up and down with excitement, I felt quite disappointed when she responded in a very practical and matter of fact way. Peggy must have heard many such stories and was not in the slightest way fazed by mine, only eager to help and to find an answer. She did tune in and kept me waiting for a response for quite some time. The answer wasn't quite what I had expected. According to Peggy there were three possibilities, at least:

firstly, she thought that the Jewish Ghost was perhaps a soul who died at the hands of the Nazis and who had been released by the healing power of my speech, or

secondly, that the young man was perhaps my sweetheart in that other life, who possibly died in a concentration camp and his soul was not able to leave this world before saying *Farewell* to me, which may have happened on the day of my speech, or... Peggy paused again for a great length of time, and said that

the third possibility was the most likely in her opinion. Holding me in suspense, she allowed for another pause and then suggested, causing a shockwave through my body, that the young Jewish man I had seen in Crewe may have been me, and that I was looking at myself in a past life, which had ended during the

Third Reich, releasing the immense trauma of that life there and then, through the power of Love, with a capital L.

In other words, I was meeting myself in another dimension. Peggy implied that she felt strongly about the third possibility. Could this be true? Have I released the *ghost* inside of me, all the pain of this and another lifetime, with my commitment to communicate (unbeknown to me at the time of the speech) with a mostly Jewish audience in Crewe about my German-Jewish dilemma?

I concluded that if this was so, if the image I saw of the young Jewish man was a reflection of myself from a previous life, possibly from my last incarnation prior to being born a German, then, and this made my hair stand up:

I clearly and most definitely would have been a Jew in my last life, and I had to come back as a German to write this book.

I would like to Pause for Reflection!

Perhaps some of the readers will intuitively have their own idea and insight as to who this young Jewish man could have been, and why only I could see him. But whoever he was, either myself in a past life or someone else who may have died in the Holocaust, his appearance changed my life and caused a major shift in my way of thinking about the possibility of reincarnation.

However, all things considered, I could have written about another past-life experience, in India for example. Thirteen visits in total to this magical country, over a period of fourteen years, opened my mind in a way I could never have imagined. I also had the chance to produce, direct and edit several documentaries about the guru and Avatar, Sai Baba, for example *The Miracle of Puttaparthi* and *Sai Baba – God on Earth?* To call this opportunity a *miracle* could be close to the truth, and possibly a story worthy of a separate book. Being the first female filmmaker to approach Sai Baba and ask for permission to make a documentary did not fit in with the ideas of many male ashram officials surrounding Sai Baba. I had to overcome, with patience and conviction, countless obstacles. It is only thanks to Sai Baba's support that I succeeded, and that was a major milestone for me in gaining self-confidence. Sadly, he died on the 24th April 2011, but his ashram is still buzzing with spiritual travellers and devotees.

As I wrote in the Indian Diary section, going to India felt like a homecoming, familiar and part of me, as though I had a past life in India at one time. I learned songs and prayers in Sanskrit and Hindi without great difficulty. I love everything Indian and never tire of the taste of curry. However, I had no direct recollection of a past life in India, unlike the previously described encounter with the Jewish Ghost. Obviously, that must have been my last life, as I was born, or reborn in 1949, not long after the Holocaust had ended.

Perhaps my past life memory will help people to understand the complexity of our soul journey. And perhaps understanding this possibility of reincarnation, we will break down barriers, prejudices and even hatred toward others, and, hopefully make space in our hearts for compassion, understanding and forgiveness.

Living in peace with the world starts with the first step, and that is living in peace with ourselves, looking at who we are fearlessly and critically, but with the eyes of Love. I can see that for some people this may sound sugary-sweet and possibly naive, but I have to say it anyway.

I want to believe that together we may be able to achieve the *impossible*, and that the force of our peaceful intentions can create a long-lasting change for all humanity. I want to believe that we, as a human race, are able to live a more harmonious life in a peaceful world, where an atrocity like the Holocaust becomes only a memory of the past, never to be repeated.

What I do wish for is the opening up of people's hearts and minds!

Encounter Between Two Worlds

My hometown, Mainz, in Germany, has become a wonderful example of Jewish/German reconciliation for me and I write this with a feeling of pride. As an example, one of its Catholic churches, St. Stephan, was heavily bombed during the last war and had lost all of its stained glass windows. It was only in the mid-1970s, that the resident vicar succeeded in winning the attention of a famous artist to help restore the church's glory. He chose the Jewish artist, Moishe Shagal, better known as Marc Chagall, who endowed St. Stephan with nearly 200 square yards, (Chagall's largest work) of biblical scenery in painted glass. Chagall worked on this project until shortly before his death in 1985. His legacy is an inspiration and a wonderful contribution to reconciliation. The beautiful windows attract an endless stream of visitors who come to reflect, meditate and experience moments of peace and calm. Whenever I return to Mainz, I make sure that I have time to visit this church, as it has become one of my favorite places of pilgrimage. I love to bathe in the heavenly blue light created by the most beautiful, breathtaking glass artwork.

St.Stephan's Church, Mainz

Chagall angel - detail of window

Another step in the direction of reconciliation, in my opinion, was the opening of a new Synagogue in Mainz in December 2010, standing on the grounds of the old Synagogue, which was destroyed by the Nazis in 1938. The shape of the building, designed by the Cologne architect Manuel Herz, is based on five letters from the Hebrew alphabet, meaning *Kiddush*, or **Holiness.**

Synagogue, Mainz, with columns from the pre-war Synagogue

Encounter Between Two Worlds

Synagogue, Mainz, Entrance

The architectural style of the building is a daring and exciting feast for the eyes and it is a wonderful place for worship. My heart was racing with excitement when I made a point of visiting the Synagogue for the first time in May 2014, on the day of *Shabbat*. Standing outside for a good while and summoning up courage to enter, I observed those who came to worship disappearing through the most amazing entrance, embellished with Hebrew letters. I took heart, said *Shabbat Shalom* and entered, following a couple of ladies upstairs to the women's section. Picking up a prayer book, I was then instructed by my friendly and welcoming neighbors as to which point had been reached in the worship. There was no way for me to follow the speed of prayers, or understand what was happening. I closed my eyes and let the sounds and atmosphere penetrate deep inside my soul. *Welcome, Louise!* To say that I felt happy would be a total understatement.

> ***I had come full circle; I had reached a point
> of deep inner peace with myself.***

The Synagogue has now, just like St. Stephan Church, become another well-loved place for me to return to. A seed for new beginnings for the Jewish-German community has been planted; there is a new hope of living in peace and harmony for future generations, a new hope for the concept of Unity in Diversity.

I started this book by calling for **World Peace,** and proposed that I would take you, the reader, with me on a journey of discovery on how to go about achieving it. Where did this journey take us? Yes, of course, I would love to be able to single-handedly stop any conflicts anywhere in the world, just like the cartoon characters Superwoman and Superman. But reality sadly limits my ability to do that and therefore my only way of making a contribution to World Peace lies in the strength I have to make peace with myself. And that amazing transformation, that miracle, might create ripples from me as an individual, to the family, into the community...and out into the world. I would like this book to create endless ripples of Peace!

During the journey of discovery, I have tried to show how the *guilty and troubled German* in me experienced a cathartic heavenly act of *Forgiveness*. It came out of nowhere and changed my life.

It gave me the freedom to live this life in a less burdened and more confident manner, having found peace within me.

I would like to remind the reader at this point about my meeting with Al Drucker, and his words that left such a deep imprint in my mind and which gave a new perspective to my experiences:

"Let me tell you something, you are not the story. Tell the story, but do not feel attached to it, that only creates pain. I felt guilty all my life. All Jews feel guilty. All Germans feel guilty. All human beings feel guilty about one thing or another. We are all born with guilt. Always remember: You are not the story. Be happy".

I am certain that I am not alone in describing my strange and at times stressful journey. Many of us don't really know who we have been or have a clear idea about who we will become. I do believe, however, that we take the awareness that we have gained in a lifetime with us, to our next life…until living is an option we get to choose, rather then being chosen for us. Until then, we come together and play our roles as assigned in our part. And the only thing we can do is to **live in the NOW, because that is all there is, this moment!**

It has been a long journey and I am still a *work in progress*, as after one challenge is met, another one pops up, but that's life, and I hope that I am ready and willing to meet all such challenges.

I thank you, the reader, for travelling with me for a while and wish you also a successful and enjoyable journey, full of laughter, joy, happiness, good health and most of all…an endless supply of

LOVE AND LIGHT AND PEACE!

19

On My Way To The Stars

On my way to the starsI have fought many wars
But I held head up high
'til I was touching the sky.

How did I do it? You may as well ask
Well, it was not always easy
To master my tasks.

I wasn't always moral - I wasn't always true
But deep inside the core of me - my inner light could always
See
A glimpse
Of the light that shone strong and bright -
that light would guide me
Where
True Love and Peace is for all to share.

I went out on a limb - believing in love
And when things toughened up
I sought help from above.

Keep going; keep loving - when troubles prevail
That was my goal

I did not want to fail.

***On my way to the stars ***I fought many wars
I did not win them all
But I'm still walking tall.

On my way to the starsI held head up high
Now I'm out of the wars
In a limitless sky.

Peace & Love, Louise Illig-Mooncie

Acknowledgments

I wish to say a big Thank You to all the wonderful people who supported me and helped me finalize my book:

* Alan (my husband) – for his never-ending support and patience and his very constructive input

* Boris (my son) – for encouraging me to write this book. For always helping me out when I needed support and for pushing me to write from the heart, without fear of exposure

* Heidi (my mother) – for telling me anecdotes about her life, the war years, her hopes and fears, her family successes and tragedies – all of which contributed to my sense of who I am, this lifetime

* Dave Patching for the wonderfully creative book cover design, turning a simple photo into a work of art!

* Messianic Jewish Publishers, 6120 Day Long Lane, Clarksville, MD 21029 for the 'Torah' quote, taken from the Complete Jewish Bible by David H. Stern. Copyright 1998. All rights reserved. Used by permission: www.messianicjewish.net

* All individuals who contributed to this book by being part of the story!

Lightning Source UK Ltd.
Milton Keynes UK
UKHW012334260219
338081UK00001B/11/P